Cracking the 2nd Grade Reading & Math

A Parent's Guide to Helping Your Child Excel in School

By Mary Juliano,
Elizabeth Ann Kahn,
and the Staff of the Princeton Review

Random House, Inc.
New York

RandomHouse.com

The Princeton Review is one of the nation's leaders in test preparation and a pioneer in the world of education. The Princeton Review offers a broad range of products and services to measurably improve academic performance for millions of students every year.

The Princeton Review is not affiliated with Princeton University or Educational Testing Service.

The Princeton Review, Inc.
2315 Broadway
New York, NY 10024
E-mail: booksupport@review.com

Published in the United States by Random House, Inc., New York

ISBN: 978-0-375-76603-9

Printed in the United States of America

9 8 7 6 5 4 3 2 1

First Edition

CREDITS

Series Editor: Casey Cornelius

Content Editor: Casey Cornelius

Development Editor: Sherine Gilmour

Production Editor: Melissa Lewis

Art Director: Neil McMahon

Senior Designer: Doug McGredy

Production Manager: Greta Blau

Production Coordinators: Leif Osgood and Elfranko Wessels

Illustrators: Doug McGredy, Tom Racine, and Tim Goldman

ACKNOWLEDGMENTS

This book would not have been possible without the contributions of a talented team of writers, editors, artists, and developers, who tackled this series with devotion and smarts.

CONTENTS

139 MATH

Introduction

You and Your Kid

Your job is to help your child excel in school. Everyone agrees that children bloom when their parents, family, friends, and neighbors nudge them to learn—from the Department of Education to the Parent Teacher Association, from research organizations known as "educational laboratories" to the local newspaper, from the National Endowment for the Arts to kids' shows on TV.

But state standards hardly make for enjoyable leisure reading, and plowing through reports on the best ways to teach math and reading can leave you with a headache, rubbing your temples. You're caught in the middle: you want to help your kid, but it's not always easy to know how.

That's where *Cracking the Second Grade* comes in. We identified the core skills that second graders need to know. Then, we put them together along with some helpful tips for you and fun activities for your kid. We built this book to be user-friendly, so you and your kid can fit in some quality time, even as you're juggling all your other parental responsibilities.

A Parent's Many Hats

As a parent, you're a cook, a chauffeur, a coach, an ally, and oh so many other things. So, keep it simple. Check out these ways you can use *Ahead of the Curve* to get involved in your child's academic life.

Teacher. You taught your kid how to cross the street and tie his or her shoes. In addition, you may have worked to teach your child academic skills by reviewing definitions, helping your child memorize facts, and explaining concepts to your child. By doing so, you are modeling a great learning attitude and great study habits for your child. You are teaching him or her the value of school.

Nurturer. As a nurturer, you're always there to support your child through tough times, celebrate your child's successes, and give your child rules and limits. You encourage your child while holding high expectations. All of this can help your child feel safe and supported enough to face challenges and opportunities at school, such as tests, projects, new teachers, and so on.

Intermediary. You are your child's first representative in the world. You're the main go-between and communicator for your child (school-to-home and home-to-school).

Advocate. As an advocate, you can do many things: sit on advisory councils at school, assist in the classroom, join the PTA, volunteer in school programs, vote in school board elections, and argue for learning standards and approaches you believe in.

· · · · · · · · · · · · · ●

Sometimes it's hard to know what to do, and it's easy to feel overwhelmed. But remember, it's not all on your shoulders. Research shows that family and close friends all have a huge effect on kids' academic success.

What's in This Book

The Skill
Each lesson targets a key second-grade skill. You and your kid can either work on all the lessons or pick and choose the lessons you want. If time is short, your kid can work on an activity without reviewing an entire lesson.

Just for You
Tips, advice, insight, and clues from parents and educators start here! Read this before diving into the rest of the lesson.

First Things First
This is the starting point for your kid in every lesson.

Supplies
Get your kid in the habit of gathering supplies before starting a lesson.

Jump Right In!
These are questions for your kid to complete independently. Give your kid as much time as he or she needs. But if your kid takes more than 30 minutes, consider the possibility that he or she may be having a hard time focusing, be unfamiliar with the skill, or have difficulty with the skill.

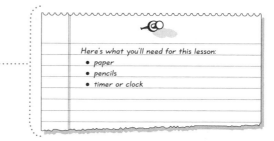

Range, Mode, and Mean

We live in a data-driven world filled with information about everything from how many people live in a certain area to who likes what flavor ice cream. We use data to make key decisions: what doctor to choose, what dinner to eat, how much to pay for things, and so on. While data is crucial, sometimes it seems our lives are dominated by data. We wonder what our kids' futures will be—strapping techno-gadgets to their brains, crunching numbers all the time, following streams of flowing data?

You know that your kids need to be comfortable understanding and using data. It's key for their lives today, and it's absolutely crucial for the future that they will be a part of creating.

By thinking about data in terms of range, mode, and mean, your child is starting to practice "viewing" data as a resource. The numbers aren't something to be memorized (there are too many numbers and sets of data in the world to memorize them all!)—the numbers are something to be understood. By having a chance to play around with range, mode, and mean, your kid can get more comfortable looking at data, pondering it, analyzing it, and even developing opinions about it.

First things first: Get a sense of what your kid already knows. Turn the page and tell your kid to Jump Right In!

Here's what you'll need for this lesson:
- *paper*
- *pencils*
- *timer or clock*

Jump Right In!

1. $3 \times 4 =$

A. 1

B. 7

C. 9

3. $6 \times 0 =$

A. 0

B. 5

Checking In
Check your kid's answers to the Jump Right In! questions. Whether your kid aced the Jump Right In! questions or had some trouble, here's stuff you can do to keep supporting your kid.

Watch Out!
These tips identify common pitfalls and help you help your child avoid them.

What to Know...
Review these key skills, definitions, and examples with your kid. Questions and tips are provided so you and your kid can talk about the skills.

Second Graders Are...
Your child's natural stages of growth can play into academic success. These tips give you insider info on the developmental stages of your child and how to help your child through his or her transitions.

Checking In

Ⓐ Answers for page 13:

1. A

2. C

3. An A+ answer: "Primates are animals such as apes, gorillas, and mo The story says that these animals are examples of primates and tha their hands and feet to hold on to things."

4. An A+ answer: "Aquatic means something that lives in the water. T says that fish and turtles are aquatic animals that live in the water

Did your child get the correct answers? If so, ask your child to point out the clues in the story that showed the meaning of the words *watch* and *sign*.

Did your child get one of the answers wrong? If so, explain to your child that *watch* and *sign* have more than one meaning. Review the answer choices to q and 2 and talk about the various meanings of the words *watch* and *sign*.

Watch Out!

Sometimes second graders try to figure out a word's meaning by using the d find the most interesting. For example, did your child select the wrong mea word "watch" in question 1? Maybe he or she was thinking about watchi

What to Know . . .

Kids use division all the time when they are sharing. Review these skills wit child this way.

- **Equal groups** are groups that have the same number of items in th

- **Division** is an operation on two numbers that tells how many grou It also tells how many items are in each group. The **division sign**

- The **quotient** is a number resulting from dividing a number by ano number. For example, in 24 ÷ 8 = 3, the quotient is 3.

Second Graders Are...
Children at this age can be focused inwardly and may ap withdrawn at times. Their ide opinions, thoughts, and feelin are important to them, and th

On Your Way to an "A" Activities

Type: Art
Materials needed: Paper, scissors, a
Number of players: 2 or more

Play "Starry, starry night." Fold a piece of paper in ha
out half of a star that includes part of the fold. When
up the paper, you'll have a whole symmetrical star. T
this time, fold the paper twice. Cut out part of a star
both folds. Try making stars with many folds. Then h
around your room!

 ## Study Right

Conducting research can help your child learn. Research symmetry
Use a folder with two pockets. Label the left pocket "Asymmetrical"
pocket "Symmetrical." Collect pictures as examples of asymmetrical
shapes. Work with your child to identify the shapes and to put them
pocket. Go through the pictures with your child and discuss why one
symmetry while another does not.

Using Your Head

Grab a **pencil** and some **crayons** or **markers**!

Read each problem. Decide if you have to add or su
the word "add" or "subtract" to show what you nee
Then, solve the problem.

How Does Your Kid Learn Best?

Did you know that your kid learns in a lot of different ways? When kids learn, they use their minds, their bodies, and their senses—sight, sound, taste, touch, and smell.

Some kids can succeed in any classroom, while others need specialized learning support, but all of them have strengths and weaknesses. Your kid can learn to rely on his or her strengths and then work on any weaknesses. This book is full of activities that address each of these learning styles.

Visually—Using Our Sense of Sight
Your kid may learn best by looking at pictures, outlines, maps, and such. Your kid may like to draw pictures or take notes.

Auditory—Using Our Sense of Sound
Your kid may learn best by listening to teachers speak, discussing with friends and classmates, and listening to music while studying. Your kid may like to tap a rhythm with his or her pen or pencil while studying.

Kinesthetic—Using Our Sense of Touch and Movement
Your kid may learn best by moving, taking action, or walking around.

How to Use Learning Styles

Talk with your child about his or her successes at school, home, or with hobbies. How did your child learn what he or she needed to succeed? Knowing how your child learns best can help you make the most of your child's natural strengths and work on your child's weaknesses.

Once you know how your child likes to learn, you can make sure your child includes those learning methods that work (especially when studying for important tests). You can also support your child as he or she tries out more challenging learning methods. In the long run, this will help your child become a well-rounded learner!

 **The Goal**

You know getting involved with your child's school experiences is the right decision. But here's a reminder of some of the rewards you may reap!

Research shows that getting involved in your kid's school experiences can result in:

- Increased academic performance

- Better behavior at school

- Increased academic motivation

- Better school attendance

And lest you think your kid reaps all the rewards, you might find that helping your child learn gives you:

- More info about your kid's school

- A greater sense of your own learning preferences

- More appreciation for all the work you did as a student

- A better relationship with your child's teacher and school staff

Want to Know More?

Check out these Web sites and organizations for more reading and math support.

Family Math and Matemática Para La Familia. If you want information about more effectively helping your child in mathematics, go to http://equals.lhs.berkeley.edu/.

MAPPS (Math and Parent Partnerships). If you want activities and mini-courses to learn about becoming more engaged in your child's school mathematics program, go to http://math.arizona.edu/~mapps/.

National Parent School Partnership (PSP) Program. If you want to better understand parental rights, the structure of schools, and how to enhance parent/teacher conferences, go to www.maldef.org/psp.

Parent Information and Resource Centers (PIRCs). If you want information about your rights under the No Child Left Behind Act as well as training, advocates, or other assistance, go to www.ed.gov/programs/pirc/index.html.

Parents for Public Schools. If you want to find out about chapters of parents working together to advocate for school improvement, go to www.parents4publicschools.com.

PTA (Parent Teacher Association). If you want to connect with other parents involved in local schools, go to www.pta.org.

Parent Training and Information Centers. If you want to find out about education and services to assist a child with disabilities, go to www.taalliance.org/centers/index.htm.

PESA (Parent Expectations Support Achievement). If you want techniques for improving your child's academic achievement, go to http://streamer.lacoe.edu/pesa/.

PIQE (Parent Institute for Quality Education). If you want to learn about how to motivate your child in school, develop a home learning environment, work with the school system, or prepare for college, go to www.pique.org.

Reading Is Fundamental. If you want help with supporting your child's reading and learning, go to www.rif.org.

Using the Structure of Words

Your kid probably has a favorite animal. He or she might love frogs more than anything in the world. The picture of a frog on the cover of a children's magazine can make your kid excited to read the article inside, which is great! But what if the article contains compound words that he or she has trouble breaking into two words? Or prefixes and suffixes that your kid isn't familiar with? There might be contractions too. If your kid becomes too frustrated or frazzled, he or she might just decide not to continue reading.

You want your kid to feel successful and confident with whatever reading materials he or she picks up. Understanding compound words, prefixes, suffixes, and contractions, as well as word families, will help your child improve his or her reading skills. Of course, this means that your child will do better in school. In addition, increased ability to understand a wide range of words and sentences will encourage your child to read for fun.

First things first: Get a sense of what your kid already knows. Turn the page and tell your kid to Jump Right In!

Here's what you'll need for this lesson:
- *index cards*
- *paper*
- *crayons or markers*
- *tape*
- *construction paper (optional)*

Jump Right In!

Can a Woodchuck Tell the Weather?

Have you ever seen an animal with <u>thick</u> brown hair? Was it larger than a mouse but smaller than a dog? Do you live in the United States or Canada? If so, you might have seen a woodchuck. They are also called <u>groundhogs</u>.

Woodchucks eat green plants. They are awake during the day and sleep at night. <u>They're</u> good at swimming, climbing, and digging. They dig a home in the ground. This home is called a burrow. This is where they <u>happily</u> sleep for the whole winter.

Some people believe that a groundhog can tell the weather. Every year on February 2, they watch a groundhog come out of its burrow. If it sees its shadow, they think there will be six more weeks of winter. This day is called "Groundhog Day."

1. The word *groundhog* is made up of what two words?

    A. round and hog

    B. ground and hog

    C. grunt and hog

    D. ground and hot

2. The word *they're* is made up of what two words?

    A. they had

    B. they have

    C. they are

    D. they do

3. The words *thick, pick,* and *stick* are in the same word family. Their endings sound the same and are spelled the same. Write three words in the same word family as *might*.

    _____

    _____

    _____

4. The word *happily* is the word *happy* with the new ending *–ly*. Change the words below to end with *–ly*.

    Swift   _____

    Quick   _____

    Slow   _____

Excellent Job!

 **Checking In**

ⒶAnswers for page 13:

> **1.** B
>
> **2.** C
>
> **3.** An A+ answer: Any three words that end in *–ight*, such as *night*, *sight*, *light*, *fight*, *flight*, *right*, *plight*, *bright*, *tonight*, or *delight*
>
> **4.** An A+ answer: Swiftly, quickly, slowly

Did your child get the correct answers? If so, ask how. For question 1, ask, "Why did you choose *ground* and *hog*?" Tell your child that a word made up of two words is called a *compound word*. Then, ask your child if he or she can find another compound word in the passage (woodchuck).

Did your child get one of the answers wrong? Review examples of compound words, contractions, word families, or prefixes and suffixes. For example, with question 1, he may not have understood what a compound word is. Give your child examples of compound words such as *baseball* and *lighthouse*. Give him examples of words that are not compound words too, such as *swimming* and *shadow*, so that he can see the difference. Then, ask him to tell you what a compound word is. If your child answered any of the other questions incorrectly, use the same approach.

 **Watch Out!**

Second graders may have trouble recognizing words and word parts because they are still developing knowledge and skills in sound-letter correspondences and the pronunciation of sounds. For example, in question 2, they may not understand what two words are used to form a contraction, and they may not remember the location or meaning of an apostrophe.

When listing words in the same family as *might* in question 3, your child might misspell a word (for example, *kight* instead of *kite*) or give you a nonsense word such as *gight*. If this happens, ask your child to use the word in a sentence and to tell you what the word means. Or, look the word up in the dictionary together to see if it's real.

What to Know...

Developing strong reading skills starts with mastering the fundamentals.

Review these skills with your child this way:

- A **base** word is the smallest unit of speech and unit of meaning.

- A **prefix** can be added to the beginning of a base word to change its meaning. Some examples: dis–, un–, bi–, tri–, and mis–.

- A **suffix** can be added to the end of a base word to change its meaning. Some examples: –full, –less.

- **Compound words** are words made up of two or more words (*football, sunburned*).

- A **word family** is a group of words that share the same ending. The ending must sound the same and be spelled the same (*new, mew, blew*).

- A **contraction** is a word formed by combining two words. Contractions are formed when some of the sounds in the words are replaced by an apostrophe ('), as in *I'm* or *isn't*.

You and your child might use a recipe like the one below.

<u>Preheat</u> the oven to 350°F.

You <u>won't</u> need milk.

Add a <u>teaspoon</u> of vanilla.

Spread the batter <u>evenly</u> in the pan.

<u>Make</u> a great <u>cake</u>!

. . . .

Ask your child to read the sentences in the recipe and find a prefix, suffix, compound word, contraction, and two words in the same word family among the underlined words. Make sure your child explains his or her answers.

 Checking In

Help your child avoid mixing up word structures. If he or she chooses the wrong word, ask your child to explain what prefix, suffix, compound word, and contraction mean. Then, tell him or her to draw a line between the parts that make up each word. For example, if your child draws a line between *pre* and *heat* in the first sentence, ask, "Is *pre* a word? Is *heat* a word? What does this tell us about the type of word that *preheat* is?

On Your Way to an "A" Activities

Type: Arts and Crafts
Materials needed: index cards, tape, construction paper (optional), markers or crayons
Number of players: 2 or more

Write each word in the Word Bank below on the bottom of an index card. Draw a picture of the word. Mix up the index cards and take turns putting words together to make compound words. Tape the words together on a larger piece of paper to make a poster!

Word Bank: home, chair, scraper, corn, fly, soft, butter, foot, note, pen, book, first, second, pig, fly, star, fish, flash, light, pop, ball, hand, fire, sun, sky, burn, light, night, time, work

Type: Game/Competitive
Materials needed: index cards
Number of players: 2 or more

Play a memory game. Write a contraction on one index card and the words that make it up on another. For example, you could write "isn't" on one card and "is not" on another. How many contractions can you think of? Then, lay the cards facedown on a table and play a memory game to find the matching cards. The player to have the most pairs at the end wins!

Using Your Head

*Grab a **pencil**!*

Finish the poem below. Circle the correct answers.

Winter Surprise

On a cold winter's day,

Three months before (<u>April</u>, <u>May</u>, <u>June</u>),   (Same word family as "day" and "play")

A groundhog wants to play.

"It's spring," she thinks,

She looks up and (<u>blinks</u>, <u>says</u>, <u>hints</u>),   (Same word family as "thinks" and "winks")

Then she climbs out and winks.

She looks to the ground,

It is her shadow she's (<u>done</u>, <u>seen</u>, <u>found</u>)!   (Same word family as "ground" and "bound")

For a six-week nap she's bound.

1. What are the missing words in the poem?

_____

_____

_____

2. What contraction fits in the sentence "_____ her shadow she's found!"?

   A. They'll

   B. Won't

   C. It's

 **Study Right**

When reading aloud with your child, practice reading with inflection. This means that as you read, vary the pitch and loudness of your voice. Also, group words that sound good together in one breath, rather than reading one word at a time in the same tone of voice. Reading text this way increases reading fluency and comprehension by giving your child more opportunities to break down difficult text. Reread this poem with your child's answers and with inflection, and then read it without inflection and ask your child which version sounded better. Ask your child to read a sentence as many different ways as he or she can think of and choose the one that sounds the best.

Second Graders Are...

Second graders often evaluate themselves and their performance both socially and academically. They may be sensitive about making mistakes and may not try new things because they're scared of failure. Present these activities in a relaxing, playful way so that your child feels safe exploring new territory.

Answers: 1. May, blinks, found; 2. C

Using Context

When you read the sentence, "A friendly cat brushed against my leg," you probably picture a cat touching a person's leg as it walked by. But your child might picture a cat actually brushing someone's leg with a hairbrush. Like many words, *brush* has several meanings. To know which meaning is intended in a sentence, readers can look for context clues in the surrounding sentences.

Second graders are still developing their reading comprehension skills. When they come across multiple-meaning words, they often stick to the meaning of the word that they already know, even if it doesn't make sense. Using the context of the sentence can help them find the correct meaning of a multiple-meaning word or find the meaning of an unfamiliar word.

First things first: Get a sense of what your kid already knows. Turn the page and tell your kid to Jump Right In!

Here's what you'll need for this lesson:
- paper
- pencils
- dictionary
- highlighter
- second-grade reading materials
- 20 index cards
- scissors

Jump Right In!

Fran's Birthday

"Where should I hide when the game starts?" Fran asked herself. For her ninth birthday, Fran had known that she wanted to have a big game of hide-and-seek. Her parents helped her plan a game at the park. Now, the day of her big game of hide-and-seek was here.

"Whoever chooses the short straw will be the finder," Fran told her friends. Henry chose the shortest straw. He started counting to 60 slowly.

Fran watched as kids hid behind rocks and trees. She wanted to find the best spot. Fran heard Henry count, "14, 15, 16." She <u>crouched</u> under a bush. She noticed Dan and Maria on the other side. "Henry will find me if he sees Dan or Maria," she thought.

Henry continued counting, "27, 28, 29." Fran ran to the baseball diamond. She didn't see any kids in the dugout. She climbed under the player's bench. Just then, she heard laughing. Cam and Nick were crouched next to her. She climbed out onto the grass.

Fran had to hide quickly. She looked left. She looked right. She looked down at the grass. Fran remembered that some animals can <u>camouflage</u> themselves by blending in with trees. They can't be seen because they look like the trees. She looked at her green <u>dress</u>. She quickly grabbed two twigs with <u>leaves</u>. Then, she laid down in the grass and put the leaves over her face and legs. She had the perfect spot!

1. In paragraph 3, *crouched* means "bent low to the ground." Which group of words helps you know this?

   A. "heard Henry count"

   B. "She noticed"

   C. "14, 15, 16"

   D. "under a bush"

2. In paragraph 5, *dress* means

   A. to put clothes on

   B. to arrange something

   C. something that is formal

   D. a piece of clothing with a skirt

3. In paragraph 5, what does the word *camouflage* mean?

   _____

   _____

4. What does the word *leaves* mean here?

   Jill always says good-bye to her teacher before she <u>leaves</u> school.

   _____

Excellent Job!

 *Checking In*

Answers for page 21:

1. D

2. D

3. An A+ answer: "*Camouflage* means to hide by looking like something else."

4. An A+ answer: "*Leaves* means that Jill goes away from school."

Did your child get the correct answers? If so, ask, "How does 'under a bush' help us understand the word *crouched*? What does it make you think of?" For question 2, make sure your child understands the different meanings of the word *dress* by coming up with sentences for each meaning.

Did your child get any of the answers wrong? If so, ask, "Why did you pick that answer?" For question 1, ask, "What would you have to do in order to hide under a bush?" For question 2, ask your child how he or she defined the word *dress* and to use it in the sentence. Tell your child to try the other choices in the sentence until he or she finds an answer that makes sense.

 *Watch Out!*

Second graders may not be used to using context clues to find the meaning of a new word. If your child sees a new word in a sentence, prompt him or her to look for context clues by asking, "What other words in the sentence can help us figure out what this word means?" If he or she has trouble finding context clues, go through each word in the sentence and ask, "What does this word tell me?" Practice this skill when you talk to your child. When your child asks you what a word means, provide a sentence using the word and encourage him or her to figure it out using only the context of the sentence.

What to Know...

Context clues can help your child find the meaning of an unfamiliar word or a word with multiple meanings.

Review these skills with your child this way:

- **Context clues** are words, phrases, and information that surround a word in a passage and help you figure out the meaning of the word.

- **Multiple-meaning words** are words that have several different meanings depending on how they are used.

You and your child might see a flier like this in your neighborhood.

Bird-Watching Class

Do you enjoy bird-watching?

<u>Spring</u> from your bed early Saturday morning.

Don't stop running until you reach the park.

We hope to catch the colorful <u>bills</u> of birds

gobbling down insects of many sizes!

The context clues "from" and "running" can help your child define the word *spring,* and the context clues "of birds" and "gobbling" can help define *bills.*

Ask your child to circle the context clues that tell him or her what the words *spring* and *bills* mean.

 *Checking In*

Kids may struggle with multiple-meaning words because they want to use the meaning they're most familiar with, even if it doesn't make sense in the context of the sentence. For example, they may say that *bills* refers to dollar bills or the bill you get at a restaurant after dinner. Encourage your child to read the sentence aloud, replacing *bills* with "checks" or "money" to see which meaning makes the most sense.

On Your Way to an "A" Activities

15 minutes

Type: Reading/Writing
Materials needed: paper, pencil
Number of players: 2

Write as many meanings as you can think of for these words: *bat, bill, brush, color, dress, fire, play, set, spring, stick, swing, tire, trunk,* and *well.* Then, use the words to write silly sentences. For example, you could write, "The elephant used her *trunk* to pick up the strange *trunk* and put it in the *trunk* of the car."

10 minutes

Type: Active
Materials needed: dictionary
Number of players: 2

Act out the meanings of words. For example, if your word is *nibble,* you could place your fingers near your mouth and move your lips quickly to show a nibble. Pick words from the dictionary or use the following words: *squawk, trunk, paint, nail, stem, stone, comb, skip,* and *squirm.* Can your partner guess your word?

 *Study Right*

If a child gets stuck on a word, encourage him or her to look up its meaning in a dictionary. Dictionaries are great tools for learning about the multiple meanings of words. Many dictionaries provide sample sentences with context clues to explain the meanings of words.

Type: Game/Competitive

Materials needed: highlighter, pencil, second-grade reading material

Number of players: 3 or more

Choose reading material that you can write on. Read a paragraph and highlight or underline words you don't know. Ask the other players to underline or highlight context clues that help define the underlined words. Each player gets a point for each context clue he or she finds. The first player to locate 10 context clues wins. Switch roles and play again with new reading materials.

Type: Game/Competitive

Materials needed: 20 index cards, scissors, pencils

Number of players: 2 or more

Play a memory game with multiple-meaning words. Cut the index cards in half to make smaller cards. Pick 20 multiple-meaning words. Here are some ideas: *bat, bill, brush, color, dress, fire, play, set, spring, stick, swing, tire, trunk,* and *well.* Write each meaning on a different index card. When a player matches two meanings of the same word, he or she gets a point. The player with the highest score wins.

Second Graders Are...

Second graders enjoy learning new words. In conversation, they have lots of ideas to share. However, they may not remember everything that the speaker says, even though they may be listening attentively. Repeat yourself or ask questions to make sure that your child understands what you are saying.

Using Your Head

*Grab a **pencil!***

Finish the sentences by writing context clues that show the meaning of the words in bold. The first one is done for you.

Enrique was so **hungry** that he *ate 37 apples and 16 pretzels!*

Because Nick is so **tall**, he _____.
  1

Cam crawled **quietly** under a bush so that

_____.
  2

Jack said that the book was **interesting** because it was

_____.
  3

We drank apple **cider** because we _____.
  4

Before Reading

You and your child are in a bookstore. There are walls and walls of books. You glance around and a book catches your eye. You know it's perfect for your child—on the cover is a picture of Mia Hamm, the soccer player, jumping in the air to score a goal. Your child loves to play soccer, and you know she'll enjoy reading about this talented player.

Without thinking about it, you just used important reading strategies: setting a purpose for reading, using prior knowledge, and making predictions. You wanted to find a book that your child would enjoy, you knew that as a soccer player your child would understand the discussion of soccer, and you predicted that the book would be about exciting soccer games. Second graders, however, are not used to applying these skills. They don't usually pay attention to book covers or titles and don't always stop to think about why they're reading a book or what might happen in the book. Setting a purpose, identifying what she already knows about a topic, and making predictions can help your child become more interested in what she's reading and help her to better understand it. When reading is active, it becomes more meaningful.

First things first: Get a sense of what your kid already knows. Turn the page and tell your kid to Jump Right In!

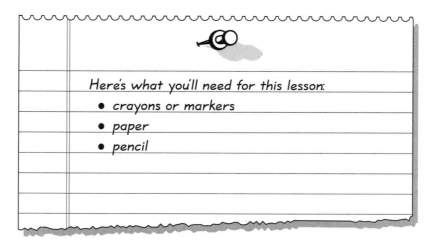

Here's what you'll need for this lesson:
- crayons or markers
- paper
- pencil

1. Read only the title of the passage below. What do you think this passage will be about?

_____

_____

Now, read the passage. Then, answer the questions.

Who Is Dr. Seuss?

The Cat and the Hat. Green Eggs and Ham. Have you heard of these books? If so, you probably know who Dr. Seuss is. His real name was Theodore Seuss Geisel. He was not a doctor, but he added Dr. to his name as a joke. His father wanted him to be a doctor.

Dr. Seuss grew up in Springfield, Massachusetts. His grandparents lived on Mulberry Street. The name of his first book is _And to Think That I Saw It on Mulberry Street_! He wrote a total of 40 children's books.

Many people wonder where he got the ideas for his books. Dr. Seuss wrote _Green Eggs and Ham_ because of a bet!

Somebody bet Dr. Seuss that he could not write a book using fifty words or less. He did it in *Green Eggs and Ham*! Some of the words are *I*, *am*, *Sam*, *do*, *not*, *like*, and *them*. Can you think of any more?

2. Why might a person read this passage?

A. to learn how to cook green eggs and ham

B. to learn how to write books

C. to learn about Dr. Seuss

D. to learn about medicine

3. Before reading the passage, it is helpful to know

A. a Dr. Seuss book

B. how to cook

C. books about ham

D. books about hats

4. What do you think happens in the book *And to Think That I Saw It on Mulberry Street*?

_____

_____

_____

_____

_____

_____

_____

Excellent Job!

 *Checking In*

Answers for pages 28 and 29:

1. An A+ Answer: "This passage will be about Dr. Seuss and his books."

2. C

3. A

4. An A+ Answer: "It's about some interesting stuff that happens on Mulberry Street."

Did your child get the correct answers? If so, ask how. Then, ask your child what he learned about Dr. Seuss. Ask your child if he knew about Dr. Seuss and his books before reading the passage. If your child did, ask if this helped him understand the passage, and how.

Did your child get any of the answers wrong? If so, ask, "Why did you pick (or write) that answer?" For questions 1 and 4, ask, "Did you make predictions based on the title and the picture, or based on what you wanted the story to be about?" If your child got questions 2 and 3 wrong, ask her to circle the words she used to choose her answers. Then, show your child that these answers are minor parts of the passage by having her circle in different colors the words that support each other answer choice. The color that shows up the most is the correct answer.

 *Watch Out!*

Sometimes second graders make predictions based on what they want or hope for in a text rather than on the details that are given. To make predictions, they should pay attention to the title, cover illustrations, or the first few lines of a text. Model how to make predictions by focusing on the details provided. For example, you might look at the cover of a mystery novel and describe what you see: "I'm looking at the picture of a man holding a magnifying glass. I think that this book may be a mystery. The man has a magnifying glass, so I predict that he's the one who tries to find something."

What to Know...

Setting a purpose for reading, using prior knowledge, and making predictions are helpful reading strategies that your kid can use before starting to read a book, story, or magazine article.

Review these skills with your child this way:

- Strong readers often set a **purpose** for reading—-they know if they are reading to get information or to have fun. To get information, people might read newspapers, instruction manuals, editorials, essays, dictionaries, or cookbooks. To have fun, people might read poems, novels, plays, or short stories.

- **Prior knowledge** is any relevant information we have before we begin reading.

- A **prediction** is an idea or thought about the future.

Your child might want to read a book like the one below.

Ask your kid what this book will be about and why he or she would want to read the book. Also ask what knowledge would be helpful to have before reading it.

Based on the title and the cover, kids might predict that this book is about:

- two kids on a journey to a place they've never been to before
- kids who go to a faraway place where there are strange creatures

Kids might give this purpose for reading:

- to have fun and enjoy an adventure story

Kids might say that knowledge of the following might be helpful:

- traveling, make-believe animals, mountains, adventure stories

 ## Checking In

Beginning readers may have trouble using before-reading strategies. So, your kid may not realize that there are different purposes for reading. He may think that readers just pick up any book or read only assigned books, like for school. To help your child set a purpose for reading, ask questions such as, "What is this book about? What can it do for you—can you learn things? Can you have fun?"

Second graders also may not realize that they can (and should) use what they already know to help them understand what they are going to read. They may think that each reading session is unrelated to the next. Remind your child that every time he or she reads, he or she gains new knowledge. Ask questions such as, "What does this book remind you of? What do you know about this subject?"

 ## Study Right

Your child may not know how to set purposes for reading, use prior knowledge, or make predictions. When you read with your child, model these behaviors. Your child will find it easier to follow concrete examples. For example, if your child picks up a book about dinosaurs, say, "There's a brontosaurus on the cover. What do we already know about this dinosaur? What do we think this book is going to say? I remember that a brontosaurus is a plant-eater. I want to learn more facts about dinosaurs. Let's read this book and see what new things we learn about dinosaurs." Make predictions based on the cover illustrations, title, chapter titles, illustrations, or even the author (if you have already read a book by that author). For example, you could say, "Jon Scieszka writes funny books. I wonder what laughs we have in store for us with this book!"

On Your Way to an "A" Activities

10 minutes

Type: Speaking/Listening
Materials needed: none
Number of players: 1 or more

Read the titles below and make predictions about these books. Explain how you came up with your predictions. Then, decide which book you would want to read first. Why?

Life on the Ocean

Dream Big

A Tale of Two Bunnies

Creepy, Crawly, Scary Creatures

20 minutes

Type: Arts and Crafts
Materials needed: crayons or markers
Number of players: 1 or more

Draw two book covers for books that people would read for fun. Then, draw two book covers for books that people would read to get information.

20 minutes

Type: Game/Competitive
Materials needed: paper, pencils
Number of players: 2 or more

Each player will write down what he or she already knows about a subject. The player who writes more will get a point. Choose your own subjects or try these: *dogs, cats, birds, firefighters, boats, dinosaurs, the Moon.*

Using Your Head

{ **5** minutes }

*Grab a **pencil**!*

Authors always have a reason for writing something. This is called the *author's purpose*. Match each book below to the author's purpose. You can use each purpose more than once.

Author's Purpose

Help you have fun

Teach you something

Make you do something

During Reading: Connections

Your child is going to a friend's birthday party. She absolutely loves ice cream cake and expects to have some at the party. To her great disappointment, your child discovers that the birthday cake is not made of ice cream! Because she is used to ice cream cake, she assumes that all the other kids must love ice cream cake too.

As kids grow, they develop more of their own feelings, thoughts, and ideas. It's wonderful to see this happen, but you want to make sure that they recognize and respect other perspectives as well. Your child made a connection between his or her own feelings (loving ice cream cake) and the outside world (the party). When reading, it's important that kids make connections between what they're reading and themselves, other texts, and the world, but they should not let their own thoughts and feelings blur what the text is saying. Making connections to the text can help readers better understand and enjoy what they're reading.

First things first: Get a sense of what your kid already knows. Turn the page and tell your kid to Jump Right In!

Here's what you'll need for this lesson:

- *paper*
- *pencils*
- *dictionary*
- *highlighters*
- *second-grade reading materials*
- *20 index cards*
- *scissors*

Clouds

Look up at the sky. You probably see white, fluffy forms moving slowly. They come in many shapes and sizes. They are clouds.

Did you know that clouds are made of tiny water drops? This is called moisture. Sometimes, the water droplets are mixed with pieces of ice.

There are three main types of clouds. Clouds that are really high up are called cirrus. They are thin and light. They look like feathers in the sky!

Clouds that are low to the ground are called stratus. These clouds are soft and gray. Clouds in the middle are called cumulus. They are thicker than cirrus clouds. They can be white globs of lines, circles, and waves.

Rain, snow, and hail fall from cumulus and stratus clouds. When a cloud is very close to the ground, it is called fog. Fog is a cloud that people can walk through!

1. You usually see clouds when you
   A. walk outside
   B. take a bath
   C. eat in your kitchen
   D. sleep in your bed

2. Which book title reminds you of this passage?
   A. *The Cat and the Hat*, by Dr. Seuss
   B. *James and the Giant Peach*, by Roald Dahl
   C. *Clouds for Dinner,* by Lynne Rae Perkins
   D. *Bunnicula*, by James Howe

3. This passage reminds me of the time when

   _____

   _____

   _____

4. This passage made me think of

   _____

   _____

   _____

   _____

Excellent Job!

Checking In

Answers for page 37:

1. A

2. C

3. An A+ answer: "This passage reminds me of when it was really cloudy outside on Monday and started raining."

4. An A+ answer: "The passage made me think about marshmallows because they are also soft and white!"

Did your child answer correctly? If so, ask, "How did you pick your answers?" Then, ask your child to tell you about a time he or she saw a cloud.

Did your child get any of the answers wrong? If so, discuss each answer choice and help your child understand which one is correct. For example, if question 1 was incorrect, ask, "Where do you see clouds? Do you think you'd have a better chance of seeing a cloud outside or in the bath, kitchen, or bedroom?" Ask your child why he or she chose his or her answer. It's possible that your child may have seen clouds of steam from the kitchen or the bathroom or seen clouds in a dream.

Watch Out!

Second graders may not be aware of what they are thinking or feeling as they are reading. When asked for their feelings about the passage in questions 3 and 4, they may just say, "I wasn't thinking of anything," even if they were thinking about clouds they've seen before. When this happens with your kid, ask him or her more specific questions about the text, such as "Have you seen clouds in funny shapes? How did that make you feel? What cloud shape would you like to see? Why? Do you remember a foggy day? Did you like the fog?" You and your child could go outside to look at clouds and relate what you see to the passage.

What to Know...

Making connections to the text can help kids understand what they're reading.

Review these skills with your child this way:

- **Text-to-self connections.** Strong readers build links and relationships between the text and their everyday lives, personal experiences, and private thoughts or feelings.

- **Text-to-world connections.** Strong readers build links and relationships between the text and the world. The link from the text connects with things they see and events going on in the world.

- **Text-to-text connections.** Strong readers build links and relationships between different parts of a text. For example, they link details from the beginning of a text to the end of a text. Strong readers also build links and relationships between texts. They link details from multiple texts, such as from a poem to a story, from a story to another story, from a story to an article, from a story to visual media (such as a picture, a movie, or an advertisement), and so on.

You and your child may see a blurb like this on the back of a book.

Oh no! Ten jellyfish are missing from the aquarium! Can Leo and Talia find them? Find out in this book about a mystery that might sting!

Ask your child how he felt or what he thought after reading each sentence. What does your kid know about jellyfish? Aquariums? Jellyfish in aquariums? Leo and Talia? Describe these questions as making connections from the text to the self, the text to the world, and one text to another.

Here are some examples of possible connections kids might make.

Text-to-Self: "I remember seeing a blue jellyfish on a beach. It looked like jelly!"

Text-to-World: "I wonder how scientists bring jellyfish to the aquarium without getting stung!"

Text-to-Text: "Leo and Talia make me think of Hansel and Gretel. I wonder if Leo and Talia are brother and sister too."

On Your Way to an "A" Activities

5 minutes

Type: Speaking/Listening
Materials needed: photos or songs
Number of players: 2 or more

Look at a photo or listen to a song. Start by saying what the photo or music makes you think about or feel. Then, see if you can make all three types of connections to the photo or song.

15 minutes

Type: Game/Competitive
Materials needed: at least 10 index cards, paper, pencil
Number of players: 2 or more

Play "Where in the World?" On each index card, write a topic, such as *turtles, musical notes, paper, bicycles, noses, sidewalks, rugs,* or your own choices. Shuffle the cards, then take turns picking an index card. Write down anything from the world that connects to this topic. Each player receives 1 point for every connection. The player with the most points wins.

Second Graders Are...

Children at this age can be focused inwardly and may appear withdrawn at times. Their ideas, opinions, thoughts, and feelings are important to them, and they like to be taken seriously. They can benefit from constant reinforcement and support of their individuality.

Type: Arts and Crafts
Materials needed: crayons or markers, pencils, paper, books or stories you enjoy
Number of players: 2 or more

While one player reads part or all of a story, the listener draws whatever he or she feels or is thinking about. The listener should try to fill an entire piece of paper with drawings. Let your hand go wherever your mind takes it!

Type: Reading/Writing
Materials needed: kid's newspaper, magazine, or Internet stories from a kid's Web site, paper and pencil
Number of players: 2 or more

On a piece of paper, make three columns with the titles "text-to-self," "text-to-world," and "text-to-text." With the other players, read a nonfiction article. Then, write your connections under each column. Which column had the most connections? Why?

Study Right

Encourage your child to stop and think about what he or she reads from time to time. You can model this for your child. Read a few pages in a book or a few paragraphs of an article and then stop. Express whatever thoughts came to you about yourself, the world, or another text.

Using Your Head

*Grab some **crayons** and a **pencil**!*

Read the poem "Peace in the Sky," then answer the questions.

Peace in the Sky

Soft, fluffy, big and white,
lots of water in the sky.
A great view from up above,
floating up so very high.

The shapes that it takes
can change with the breeze.
A house or a cat,
hanging over the trees.

It's my calm, it's my peace
when a day gets too loud.
It's a wonderful thing,
and it is a cloud.

1. Draw what the poem made you think of.

2. What books, poems, magazines, movies, or pictures does this poem make you think of? Why?

Checking Understanding

It can be very easy for a beginning reader to be confused by what he or she just read. Beginning readers are still developing their decoding and fluency skills. They may have trouble understanding what they're reading and not know what to do about it. They may not even realize that their understanding has broken down. If they do realize that they're lost and confused, they may become frustrated and give up.

Good readers picture the story and check understanding by asking questions about the text and about their own reading experience. These skills help kids clarify what they're reading and can ensure that they have successful reading experiences.

First things first: Get a sense of what your kid already knows. Turn the page and tell your kid to Jump Right In!

Here's what you'll need for this lesson:
- *paper*
- *pencils*
- *crayons or markers*
- *books*

The Fox and the Grapes

A fox walked through a farm one hot summer day. He saw some grapes hanging from a tree.

"I'm so thirsty," he thought. "Those grapes are just what I need!" He ran and jumped at the grapes, but he missed them. He tried again.

"One, two, three," the fox counted. He jumped up, but he missed the grapes again. He tried several more times, but he never caught the grapes. He gave up.

The fox was leaving the farm when he passed a cat.

"How are the grapes?" asked the cat. "I'm sure they are sour," said the fox glumly.

"Oh, that's too bad," said the cat. "I guess I won't climb up and get some for us." The cat ran away before the fox could tell the truth.

1. Picture the story in your mind. Where is the fox?

   A. on sand

   B. on snow

   C. in a tree

   D. on grass

2. Why didn't the cat get some grapes?

   A. because cats can't climb trees

   B. because the fox said they were sour

   C. because cats don't like grapes

   D. because the fox ate them all

3. Write a question you have about the story.

   _____

   _____

4. Picture the story in your mind. What does the farm look like?

   _____

   _____

   _____

Excellent Job!

Checking In

Ⓐ Answers for page 45:

    1. D

    2. B

    3. An A+ answer: Any question your child has, such as "Why did the fox say that the grapes were sour?"

    4. An A+ answer: "There is a barn, lots of fields with grass, a plow, animals, trees, and soil."

Did your child get the correct answers? If so, ask your child what words in the story helped him or her answer the questions.

Did your child get any of the answers wrong? If so, go over the incorrect answers. Tell your child, "That's an interesting idea. How do you know that is true?" Ask your child to reread the story and to underline words that tell what the fox is doing or where he is or what the cat says about the grapes. If your child claims not to have questions about the story, ask him some specific questions, and then have him retell the story to you.

Watch Out!

Sometimes second graders are not aware that they are confused or have misunderstood something. If you notice that your kid has misunderstood a part of the story, say, "That part was confusing. Let's go back and read it again and pay attention to the background in the story." Remind your kid that all readers (adults included) sometimes get confused when they read. When good readers feel confused, they go back and reread parts or the whole story to make sure everything makes sense.

What to Know...

Picturing the story and checking understanding can help your child understand what he or she is reading.

Review these skills with your child this way:

- **Picture the story.** Strong readers develop their comprehension by picturing the story (imagining the details and the actions) as they read.

- **Check understanding and clear up confusion.** Strong readers check their understanding. They ask themselves questions before they read, while they read, and after they read. When strong readers identify that they are confused, they take the time to answer their questions before they continue reading, and they use details from the story whenever possible.

You and your child might see a poster like this in your neighborhood.

Missing Cat!

My cat, Isabella, was last seen Friday on the farm. She has orange, brown, and white stripes. Isabella weighs about 12 pounds and is very friendly. Please call Isaac if you find her.

Ask your child to picture in his or her mind what Isabella looks like. Then, ask your child how he or she came up with the picture.

Good readers picture in their minds what they are reading. This shows that they understand what they've read. A good, detailed description of the missing cat from the poster is "I picture a medium-sized cat with orange, brown, and white stripes. I imagine her running around haystacks and rubbing against a farmer's leg because she is friendly."

Good readers ask themselves questions before, during, and after they read. They ask questions about the text, such as:

- What just happened?

- How do I know that?

- Why did the character do that?

- What is the character feeling right now?

In addition, good readers ask themselves questions about their own reading experience, such as:

- How do I feel right now?

- Do I know what is going on?

- Do I like the story?

- Have I ever felt the same way?

If good readers are confused, they reread the passage. If they don't understand a word, they look for context clues, use a dictionary, or ask a parent, teacher, or friend.

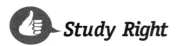 ## Study Right

Rereading is an excellent way to check for understanding. Even if your child doesn't have trouble with a book, she can reread it. Readers often discover something new each time they read something. For example, a reader might miss an author's description of a place the first time around, or not realize that a character says something funny or strange. If the story has dialogue, change your voice for the characters each time. Encourage your child to do the same.

On Your Way to an "A" Activities

 **10 minutes**
Type: Active
Materials needed: a book
Number of players: 2 or more

Read a story from a book or read the story below. Then, figure out if you have any questions about the story. Next, act it out— see if acting it out answers your questions!

Henry jumps over a log. Then, he climbs up a ladder and slides down a slide. He jumps on one foot, then on the other foot. He climbs the stairs to the top of the fort. He looks all around him. He can see the entire playground from up there. He climbs down slowly so nobody can hear him. Then, he races to the finish line and shouts, "Hooray!" He completed the obstacle course! He gives high fives to all his friends.

 **20 minutes**
Type: Arts and Crafts
Materials needed: crayons or markers, pencils, paper, books
Number of players: 1 or more

Read or listen to a story and draw a picture of a part that you liked. If someone is reading the story to you, don't look at the pictures. Instead, picture the story in your mind, and then draw what you pictured. You are the new illustrator!

Has your child breezed through the activities? If so, he or she can work on this Using Your Head activity independently.

Using Your Head

Grab a **pencil**!

Match the letter of the question to the line or lines in the poem that answers it.

    A. What living things are in this poem?

    B. What do people and animals share?

    C. What word rhymes with *alive*?

    D. How should people treat the Earth?

Life on Earth

1. Oh, the Earth is so alive,
2. With people and birds that dive,
3. Air, water, apples, and grapes,
4. Animals and plants of many shapes,
5. All together, we must share this beautiful Earth,
6. And remember to treat it with care!

After Reading

Have you ever asked your child what he or she did in school and received an answer that goes on and on and on? It's great that your child is using lots of details and sharing his or her thoughts. However, this natural tendency of kids to include every little detail can make writing summaries a challenge.

Summarizing a story is an important skill. A summary includes only the most important details of a story in a sentence or two. When children retell the main ideas of a text in their own words, they show that they understand what they are reading. Many times, however, second graders become lost in the details of a story and miss the bigger picture. While paying attention to details is important, good readers learn to use only the most important details to form summaries of what they read.

First things first: Get a sense of what your kid already knows. Turn the page and tell your kid to Jump Right In!

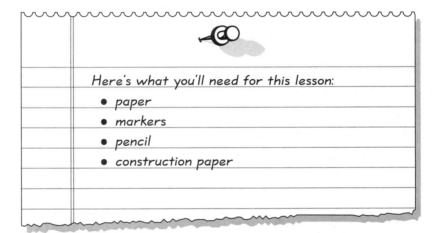

Here's what you'll need for this lesson:

- paper
- markers
- pencil
- construction paper

Summer to Fall

Dan loved to paint. He liked to lay all his paints out on the table. He liked to paint on big pieces of paper and use brushes of different sizes. One time, he didn't know what to paint. So, he looked around his room. Then, he looked out his window. "I'll try painting that maple tree over there," he said to himself.

Dan mixed some blue, yellow, and red paint. He painted a tree trunk with branches that spread out in all directions. "Now it's time for some leaves," he decided. So, he picked up a thin brush. Then, he mixed some yellow and blue to make green. He used this green to paint the leaves on the branches.

He'd spent a while on his painting. It was late in the day and the sun was setting. Quickly, he mixed some yellow and red to make orange for the sunset. He dipped a medium-sized brush into the new color and held it over the paper. Suddenly, he heard a loud "ca-caw!" sound. A crow was flying by the window. He looked up from his painting to watch it.

While he looked at the crow, some orange paint dripped onto the painting. "Oh no, my green leaves are now orange," he said. "Wait! In the fall, the leaves on this tree will be yellow, orange, and red. I'll create a maple tree in the fall!" Dan added orange, yellow, and red leaves. After he added a final leaf, he looked at his painting. "Who knew a drip of paint could be so helpful," he smiled.

1. Choose the best summary of paragraph 1.

    A. Dan began painting a tree.

    B. Dan painted a tree on the wall.

    C. Dan set up his paints and mixed some colors.

    D. Dan set up his paints and decided to paint a tree.

2. What colors did Dan mix to make orange?

    A. blue, yellow, and red

    B. yellow and red

    C. red and green

    D. yellow and blue

3. What did Dan want to use the orange paint for?

    _____

    _____

4. Write a summary for paragraph 4 in your own words.

    _____

    _____

    _____

Excellent Job!

 *Checking In*

Answers for page 53:

1. D

2. B

3. An A+ answer: "Dan wanted to paint the sunset with his orange paint."

4. An A+ answer: "Dan dripped orange paint on the green leaves. He decided to change his painting to a tree in the fall."

Did your child get the correct answers? If so, tell your child to underline the details that he or she used to create the summary. Ask your child to explain what a *summary* is.

Did your child get any of the answers wrong? If so, have him or her reread each paragraph and tell you the main point in his or her own words. Write down the main points as your child states them. Have your child make a summary using the notes, and then ask him or her to match the summary to the correct answer choice.

 *Watch Out!*

Children at this age can become lost in the details of a text. They may have difficulty picking out the most important information for a summary. They may want to include all the details they find, or they may want to include only a few details. If your child has difficulty figuring out which details to include, tell him or her to describe each paragraph using only one sentence.

What to Know...

Whenever kids tell someone what a book, movie, or television show is about, they are using details to make a summary.

Review these skills with your child this way:

- A **detail** is a piece of information in a passage, given in a word or phrase.
- A **summary** is a retelling of the most important information in a passage or the main points of a story. A summary includes the topic, the major events, the main theme or idea, and the most important characters. A summary is usually brief.

Your child might follow these instructions about painting in art class at school.

Paint Setup

- Take a tray and sponge.
- Choose your brushes and paints.
- Fill a container with water.

Ask your child which details are most important. Then, tell him or her to summarize the directions in his or her own words.

Paint Cleanup

- Place leftover paints on the table.
- Empty the containers.
- Clean your brushes, sponge, and tray.
- Place the painting on the drying rack.

Kids should use the details to give a summary like "For setting up, we have to get out the things we need. For cleaning up, we wash everything and hang our paintings to dry."

 *Checking In*

Second graders may confuse details from their own experiences with details that they've read. Your child may use a different cleanup process at school and may mention it. If this happens, ask, "Where are those details in this text?" Then, remind your child that to summarize the text, she can use only the details in the text.

On Your Way to an "A" Activities

 10 minutes
Type: Active
Materials needed: none
Number of players: 2

Do an activity at home—alphabetize your books, build a castle with blocks, or draw a picture. Pay close attention to the steps in your activity. When you are finished, give an adult, sibling, or friend a summary of what you did. Next, ask someone to give you a summary of one of their activities, like making dinner, driving to work, or playing a game!

20 minutes
Type: Arts and Crafts
Materials needed: book, newspaper or magazine article that you enjoy reading, crayons or markers, pencils, paper
Number of players: 1 or more

Read a paragraph or page in a book, magazine, or newspaper. Write a summary in one or two sentences in the middle of the paper. All around your summary, draw pictures of the details in the paragraph.

 *Study Right*

Encourage your child to jot down important words or phrases as he or she reads. Then, ask your child to summarize from his or her own notes.

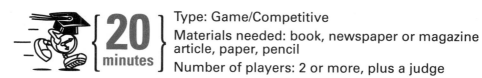

Type: Game/Competitive
Materials needed: book, newspaper or magazine article, paper, pencil
Number of players: 2 or more, plus a judge

One player should pretend to be a judge. The other players should read a book or an article from a newspaper or magazine. Then, each player writes the best summary he or she can. Take your summaries to the judge. The judge decides which summaries include the most important information. These summaries get a point!

Type: Speaking/Listening
Materials needed: paper and pencil
Number of players: 2 or more

Each player has to come up with a summary of a well-known activity, game, sport, or television show. The summaries should be three sentences or less. Players can make notes to help them write their summaries. Then, players take turns saying their summaries. The first player says his or her summary. The other players have to guess what is being summarized. The first player earns a point for every time another player guesses correctly. Now, a different player can say his or her summary. First player to get 5 points wins!

Second Graders Are...

Second graders enjoy being read to. There are a lot of books that may be too advanced for them to read, but they can still understand the text if you read to them.

Using Your Head

Grab some **crayons** or **markers** and a **pencil**!

Read the poem. Summarize it in one sentence. Then, draw a picture of your summary next to the poem!

Swish, swish, slides my brush,
red, yellow, blue, and green.
Swish, swish, glides my brush,
orange, violet, pink between.

Back and forth, up and down,
colors mix and blend.
Shapes floating all around,
overlapping without end.

Swish, swish, sun and moon,
oceans full of blue.
Swish, swish, star, and moon—
look what I've painted just for you!

Answer: The speaker used many colors and shapes to paint a sun, moon, and star for someone.

Using Illustrations

Reading is a multifaceted experience. We don't just read the words in a book; we read the photographs, illustrations, numbers, diagrams, and other visual elements on a page. Any time we interpret something symbolically, we are reading. Using illustrations to improve comprehension is an important aspect of reading, especially for young children.

Children receive a lot of reading instruction in school. This is a good thing, of course, but because second graders are so focused on reading words, sometimes they can get the false idea that reading is about only the text that's printed on the page. As a result, your child may not value the information she gets from the photographs or illustrations as highly as she values the printed text. Good readers consider everything provided for them by the authors to form a balanced interpretation of what they read.

First things first: Get a sense of what your kid already knows. Turn the page and tell your kid to Jump Right In!

Here's what you'll need for this lesson:
- *paper and pencil*
- *book with pictures*
- *crayons or markers*
- *scissors*
- *tape*
- *book with pictures*
- *hanger*
- *shoebox (optional)*
- *string*
- *3-D craft objects like beads, yarn, and felt*

Jump Right In!

The Wind and the Sun

One day, the Wind and the Sun were arguing. "I am stronger than you," said the Wind. "No, I am stronger than you," said the Sun. "How are we going to decide who is the strongest?" asked the Wind.

"I see a way to solve our argument," said the Sun. "Whoever can get the traveler to take off his jacket will be the strongest. You go first, Wind."

"I give up," said the Wind. "I'm tired. I guess it's your turn, Sun."

Then, the sun blazed down. "Well, you are the strongest, Sun," said the Wind. "You were also kinder to the traveler."

1. The wind tries to get the jacket off the traveler by

   A. knocking it off his back

   B. blowing at him really hard

   C. making it rain

   D. throwing leaves at him

2. The sun tries to get the jacket off the traveler by

   A. making the air hot

   B. telling the birds to fly by

   C. giving him a suntan

   D. smiling at the traveler

3. How did the story end?

_____

_____

4. How did the illustrations help you answer questions 1, 2, and 3?

_____

_____

Excellent Job!

 *Checking In*

Ⓐ Answers for page 61:

1. B

2. A

3. An A+ answer: "The Wind told the Sun that the Sun was stronger and kinder."

4. An A+ answer: "Part of the action in the story was in the pictures. If you didn't look at the pictures, you wouldn't know that the Wind tried to blow the jacket off the traveler or that the Sun made the traveler hot so he would take off his jacket."

Did your child get the correct answers? If so, ask your child if she can think of other books, stories, or texts she's read where she had to use the pictures. Ask her if she can find any examples at home (like maps, the backs of cereal boxes, or other examples).

Did your child get any of the answers wrong? If so, have him or her reread the text and look at the pictures more closely. Maybe your child relied only on the words for the answers. You can say, "When a story or passage has illustrations, they are part of the story too. This story is told using both words and illustrations."

 *Watch Out!*

Sometimes, second graders don't realize that illustrations and words go together in the telling of a story. Some kids look at pictures just for fun; if they look at illustrations at all, they focus only on a small detail in the illustration. For example, in the first illustration, the child might have looked only at the traveler's blowing hair, not seeing that the Wind was trying to blow off the traveler's jacket. In this story (and in many books that second graders read), illustrations show details that are not mentioned in the text of the story.

To help your child understand this, find a book, a manual with instructions, or a kid's magazine article with pictures or diagrams. Look at the pictures together. Ask questions such as, "What do the pictures show? Would you understand this story without the pictures? Why do you think the authors included the pictures?"

What to Know...

Making use of illustrations can help a reader better understand what he or she reads.

Review this skill with your child this way:

- **Illustrations** often show topics and events from a passage. Strong readers use illustrations to make sure they understand what is going on in the passage. They identify details in illustrations and answer questions based on the details in illustrations. Strong readers understand that illustrations and passages go hand in hand and that sometimes illustrations show details not mentioned in the passage.

You and your child might see these instructions inside a game of checkers.

Directions

1. Open the checkerboard and lay it flat.

2. Fill up the first three rows. Place black checkers on the black squares.

3. Fill up the last three rows. Place red checkers on the black squares.

Watch Out!

A child might have a difficult time explaining the directions without looking at the illustration. He or she might stumble over his or her words, make errors, or leave out steps. Encourage your child to always look at illustrations carefully.

Tell your child to read the directions and look at the art. Then, cover up the art with your hand. Ask your child what information is missing. Then, move your hand to show the art and cover up the directions. Again, ask your child what information is missing.

On Your Way to an "A" Activities

Type: Game/Competitive
Materials needed: book with pictures, paper, pencil
Number of players: 2 or more

Open up the book to a picture. Look closely at the picture and find as many details as possible in the picture. The player who finds the most details wins. Play the game 4 times, each time with a different picture.

Type: Reading/Writing
Materials needed: photo album or a book with only pictures, pencils, paper
Number of players: 1 or more

Look at photos in a photo album. Talk about what is happening in the photos. Write a short story about the photographs. Create words for the story based on the pictures.

 **Study Right**

Many picture books at the second-grade level have few words and detailed pictures that require readers to "read the pictures." If you and your child are reading together, do a "picture walk" and flip through the book and look only at the pictures. See if you and your child can make predictions and get a sense of the story just by looking at the illustrations. Then, go back and read the book. As you read, make sure to pause to discuss the illustrations.

Type: Arts and Crafts

Materials needed: book, one hanger, scissors, tape, string, crayons or markers, other 3-D craft objects like beads, yarn, and felt, shoe box (optional)

Number of players: 1 or more

Read a story that you enjoy and pay attention to the illustrations. Make a mobile of a favorite scene or event from the story. Draw characters and props on paper and cut them out. Tie a string at the top, and hang them from the hanger using tape. You may copy an illustration from the story and make it 3-D, or you can make up your own scene. You could also make a diorama by making a 3-D scene inside a shoe box.

Type: Speaking/Listening

Materials needed: book with print and illustrations, paper, tape

Number of players: 2 or more

Using paper and tape, cover up the print in a story. Now, tell the story by looking only at the illustrations and describing what you see.

Second Graders Are...

As second graders grow and change mentally and physically, they can benefit from and tend to prefer quiet, uncluttered work areas. Try to limit any distractions including noise, visual distractions like the television, and physical distractions, such as a lot of toys or boxes under a table.

Has your child breezed through the activities? If so, he or she can work on this Using Your Head activity independently.

Using Your Head

{ **20** minutes }

*Grab a **pencil**!*

Read the sentences and look at the pictures. Draw a line to connect the sentence to the picture it matches.

1. A gust of wind blew off Felipe's cap.

2. The sun set behind the hills.

3. Felipe had no wind to fly his kite.

4. Felipe enjoyed the sun shower.

A.

B.

C.

D.

Answers: 1. D; 2. B; 3. A; 4. C

Fiction and Nonfiction

Your child reads a lot of different books and stories. For example, your child might read a story about a boy whose family moves their home from the Moon to Jupiter, and soon your child is asking if you can move to Jupiter too! To most of us, it is obvious that this book is fictional. We take for granted that everyone knows the difference between made-up stories and real accounts. But for your child, reading is still very new and challenging, and figuring out whether the words of the story are true or made up is a completely new skill. Its importance cannot be underestimated.

All writing can basically be broken down into two essential categories: fiction and nonfiction. Because the purposes of these two types of writing differ—usually to entertain versus to inform—it's critical that your child understands the distinctions. Otherwise, it's possible that he or she can interpret a fictional account as factual, distorting his or her sense of reality. Both fiction and nonfiction are important, of course, but their purposes are truly maximized only when the reader knows what he or she is reading.

First things first: Get a sense of what your kid already knows. Turn the page and tell your kid to Jump Right In!

Here's what you'll need for this lesson:
- *15-20 books*
- *crayons or markers*
- *paper*

Fly to the Moon

It may be hard to believe that people have been to the Moon, but people have actually walked on it. We have driven a car on it. We have even played golf on the Moon! How did this happen?

In 1961, Russia flew a person into space. This had never been done before. The United States wanted to send a person into space too, but we wanted to do it better. We wanted to send a person to the Moon! President Kennedy said we could go to the Moon by 1970. He was right!

On July 16, 1969, a rocket left Earth. It flew toward the Moon. That is about 240,000 miles away. It would take years to ride a bike that far, but the rocket was fast! It took a few days to fly. Three men landed on the Moon on July 20, 1969.

The first person to step on the Moon was Neil Armstrong. He spent two hours on the Moon. Buzz Aldrin was the next person on the Moon. Other people went to the Moon too. In total, 12 people walked on the Moon. Alan Shepard even hit a golf ball on the Moon!

The last person went to the Moon in 1972.

1. Is this story true or is it made up? How do you know?

_____

_____

_____

2. Write three things you learned from this story.

_____

_____

_____

_____

3. Now write a fictional story about the Moon.

_____

_____

_____

_____

_____

_____

_____

_____

_____

_____

_____

Excellent Job!

 *Checking In*

❶Answers for page 69:

    1. An A+ answer: "The story is true. I know because it tells details about real people and real things."

    2. An A+ answer: Your child should write three facts from the story, such as "Russia flew a person into space in 1961. Neil Armstrong was the first person to step on the Moon. Alan Shepard hit a golf ball on the Moon."

    3. An A+ answer: A fictional story about the Moon

Did your child get the correct answers? If so, ask him to explain how he knew the story was nonfiction. Make sure your child understands that the entire passage was based on things that really happened.

Did your child get any of the answers wrong? If so, go over the incorrect answers. For question 1, tell your child that the entire passage is based on things that really happened. Ask your child, "Did you know that these things really happened?" If your child didn't know, explain that he or she could still figure out that the passage was nonfiction because there was nothing unbelievable in the passage. Also, the passage mentioned real places like Russia and the United States. These are clues that the passage is nonfiction. Tell your child to go back to the passage and underline the sentences that helped him or her answer each question.

 *Watch Out!*

Second graders may confuse fictional stories they have heard with nonfiction accounts. Your child may have read fantastic stories of science fiction and astronauts exploring the galaxy and may think that every story about space and astronauts is made up. Help your child learn to separate fact from fiction by emphasizing that fiction can have some facts in it, but it also has made-up details. On the other hand, nonfiction has only facts and things that really happened. If your kid isn't sure if a passage is fiction or nonfiction, work together to verify the information given. Nonfiction passages like "Fly to the Moon" are real because they tell about real people in actual times. Compare this passage to the fictional passage your child wrote about the Moon and discuss the differences.

What to Know...

Kids can have trouble differentiating between fiction and nonfiction.

Review these skills with your child this way, stressing the words in italics:

- **Fiction** is writing that tells a *made-up* story. Fiction tells a story with *imagined* characters and events. Stories and fairy tales are examples of fiction.

- **Nonfiction** is writing that tells only *facts* and *true* information. Textbooks are examples of nonfiction.

You and your child might come across the passage below in a storybook.

Playing Spaceball on the Moon

Felipe loved it on the Moon! He could see Earth from the Moon. He had lots of friends at the giant Moon station. He loved playing spaceball in the Moon's many craters.

Then, his dad said the family had to move to Jupiter. That was so far away! He didn't have any friends there. Who would he play spaceball with? Would they even *know* spaceball there?

Felipe was a star at spaceball. He was better than any human. He was as good as most aliens too. Felipe hoped he could play spaceball on Jupiter. Maybe he could learn a new game there too.

· · · · · · · · · · · · ●

Ask your child if this passage is fiction or nonfiction. Tell him or her to circle sentences that are facts and to underline sentences that are make-believe.

Good readers should recognize the following made-up details from the passage:

- Felipe had friends on the giant Moon station.

- He played spaceball on the Moon.

- His family was moving to Jupiter.

- Felipe could play spaceball better than aliens.

Good readers should recognize the following facts from the passage:

- People can see Earth from the Moon.

- The Moon has many craters.

- Jupiter is very far away from the Moon and from Earth.

 ## Checking In

A child who has difficulty distinguishing between fiction and nonfiction may mix up some of the examples above.

If your kid isn't sure if a detail is real or made up, ask him or her to consider if it could really happen. Ask questions, such as, "Do you think kids play spaceball on the Moon? Have you ever seen it? Do you know anyone who plays it? Where could we look this up?" Encourage your kid to pay attention to the title, cover, and any illustrations in a story to see if they give any hints.

Make sure that your child knows that there is nothing wrong with make-believe stories. It is not *dishonest* because the writer is not pretending that the words are true. Your kid should be clear that there is a distinction, however. Telling a story that is *supposed* to be nonfiction—but contains made-up details—is not acceptable.

 ## Study Right

When talking about fiction and nonfiction, it is helpful to think about an author's purpose. An author decides his or her purpose for writing before writing. When identifying fiction and nonfiction, ask your child what he or she thinks the author's purpose for writing is—to inform a reader about facts or to make the reader have fun?

On Your Way to an "A" Activities

Type: Game/Competitive
Materials needed: none
Number of people: 2

Think of a subject that you like. Say a sentence about it that is made up. Then, the other player has to say a sentence about it that is a fact. Switch turns. The player who says the most sentences correctly wins.

Type: Game/Competitive
Materials needed: none
Number of people: 2

Find a bookshelf with a lot of books. Sort them by fiction and nonfiction. Put all the fiction books on the left. Put all the nonfiction books on the right. How did you decide which was which?

Type: Arts and Crafts
Materials needed: crayons or markers, paper
Number of people: 1 or more

Make your own book covers for nonfiction and fiction books that you've read. The nonfiction book covers can have facts from the books. The fiction book covers can have pictures of what happens in the books.

Using Your Head

{ 15 minutes }

*Grab a **pencil**!*

Circle the sentences that are facts. Underline the made-up sentences.

1. The girl jumped over the sun.

2. Alaska is the biggest state in the United States.

3. Some people have snakes for pets.

4. My cat can fly.

5. George spoke with his dog on the phone.

6. Some animals live on land and in water.

7. Julia turned into a pumpkin.

Answers: Sentences 2, 3, and 6 should be circled. Sentences 1, 4, 5, and 7 should be underlined.

Main Idea

A class of second graders may read the same passage about the solar system and find several different main ideas. One kid might say that the passage is mostly about Saturn's beautiful rings. Another kid might say that the passage is mostly about how hot Venus is. Who's right? It may turn out that neither is—the passage is mainly about the observations of a space shuttle. Saturn's rings and Venus's temperature are just interesting details.

These kids focused on a bit of information that appealed to them instead of looking for the main point of the entire passage. You want your kid to enjoy reading and learning about things, but your kid shouldn't focus so much on the little details that the bigger picture is lost. To find the main idea, kids have to use these fun, interesting details *and* look for a statement that gives the main point of the entire passage.

First things first: Get a sense of what your kid already knows. Turn the page and tell your kid to Jump Right In!

Here's what you'll need for this lesson:
- poster board or construction paper
- crayons or markers
- pencil
- scissors
- paper
- hole puncher
- string

Jump Right In!

The Story of Rosa Parks

Rosa Parks was born in Alabama, in the southern part of the United States. She was born in 1913. At the time, there were many unfair laws that made life hard for African Americans. One law said that they could ride only in the back of a bus, not the front.

Rosa Parks believed that all people should be equal. Rosa Parks did not want to have to sit in the back of the bus just because she was African American. So one day in 1955, she sat in the front of the bus. The bus driver asked her to give up her seat, but she did not. She believed that the color of her skin should not matter.

Soon, many people of all colors refused to take the bus. The bus had to change its rules. This was the beginning of many changes. The Civil Rights Movement worked to make all people equal. Rosa Parks is a civil rights hero.

1. What is paragraph 1 mainly about?

    A. Alabama is in the southern part of the United States.

    B. Rosa Parks was born in 1913.

    C. Life was very different in 1913.

    D. When Rosa Parks was born, there were unfair laws.

2. What is paragraph 2 mainly about?

    A. Rosa Parks believed that all people should be equal.

    B. Rosa Parks did not like riding buses.

    C. The bus company changed its rules.

    D. The bus driver asked Rosa Parks to sit in the back of the bus.

3. Write three details from the story.

    _____

    _____

    _____

    _____

4. What is this passage mainly about? Use your own words.

    _____

    _____

Excellent Job!

 *Checking In*

Answers for page 77:

1. D

2. A

3. An A+ answer: "Rosa Parks did not give up her seat. This story happened in 1955. Unfair laws affected buses."

4. An A+ answer: "Rosa Parks refused to sit in the back of the bus and helped change unfair laws."

Did your child get the correct answers? If so, ask your child to explain how he or she knew what each paragraph was mainly about. Make sure your child got the right answer because he or she understood the main idea (and didn't guess).

Did your child get any of the answers wrong? If so, go over the incorrect answers. Ask your child to circle the sentence or sentences in the passage that each answer choice comes from. Then, ask your child, "Which sentence tells the most important part of the paragraph (or passage) the best?" If your child has trouble identifying details, explain that a detail is a little piece of information that supports the most important part of the paragraph (or passage).

 *Watch Out!*

Second graders may have a hard time understanding the difference between main idea and summary. Explain that a main idea is a sentence that tells the most important idea of a passage. A summary includes all the important ideas of a passage and can be longer than one sentence. Also point out that a main idea is sometimes the first or last sentence of a paragraph. Other times, the main idea isn't even stated directly.

What to Know...

The terms *main idea* and *detail* may be new to your child.

Review these skills with your child this way:

- A **main idea** is a statement of what a passage is mostly about. Often, an author states the main idea in the first or last sentence of the passage. However, an author may state the main idea anywhere in the passage. An author may choose not to state the main idea directly, in which case the reader has to infer the main idea of the passage.

- **Details** are bits of information in a passage, sometimes given in a word or a phrase. A supporting detail is a detail from the passage that supports the main idea. Sometimes, there are details in a passage that contradict the main idea.

You and your child might read this passage in a book.

The Best Gift

Elana wanted to buy a nice gift for her grandfather. He was turning 80 years old, but Elana did not know what to get him.

On his birthday, Elana walked to the nursing home where her grandfather lived. The nurses were setting up a party in the den. Elana asked to help. She blew up balloons. She taped decorations to the wall. She set up games. She even made a cake!

Then, Elana's grandfather came into the den. He looked so happy! He saw Elana and gave her a big hug. He told her that she had given him the best gift ever.

· · · · · · · · · · · · ·

Ask your child to tell you the main idea of this passage. Then, ask your child to tell you some details that helped her know the main idea.

Checking In

Instead of main ideas, kids might accidentally provide details, such as "Elana didn't know what to get her grandfather" or "Elana wanted to get her grandfather something special." If your child gives a detail instead of the main idea, try to get him or her to recognize that it is only one part of the story. Ask, "Will someone who has not read the story understand what the story is mainly about from what you just said?"

Asking your child to consider why the author wrote a passage can be a lead-in to recognizing the main idea. Ask simply, "Why do you think the author wrote this?" In the case of this story, your child might give the following main idea: "To show that you don't always have to give a present to say 'Happy Birthday!'"

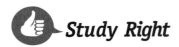

Study Right

Remind your child that there are many different ways to tell the main idea of a story. The exact words may not matter. Getting the point across is what is important.

On Your Way to an "A" Activities

Type: Arts and Crafts

Materials needed: poster board or construction paper, scissors, hole punch, string, your favorite book, crayons or markers

Number of players: 1 or more

Make your own main idea bookmark. Cut a piece of poster board or construction paper in the shape of a bookmark. Punch a hole in the top of the bookmark. Tie a piece of string in the hole. Then, look through your favorite book and decide what the main idea of it is. Write it on the bookmark. Decorate the bookmark.

Type: Reading/Writing

Materials needed: pencils, paper

Number of players: 2 or more

With another player, create stories from main ideas. Think of a brief, fun main idea, such as, "A bear makes friends with a mouse" or "A girl works hard to become a great basketball player." This will be the main idea of the story. The other player will write a short story using your main idea. All the details of the story will have to support this main idea. Trade roles and use your friend's main idea to write your story.

Using Your Head

{**10** minutes}

*Grab a **pencil**!*

Below are the main ideas of each paragraph from "The Best Gift." Match each main idea to the details that support it.

Main Ideas

1. Elana had a problem.

2. Elana did a lot to set up the party.

3. Elana's grandfather was happy about his birthday party.

Details

A. Elana didn't know what to get her grandfather for his birthday.

B. Elana blew up balloons.

C. Grandfather gave Elana a big hug.

D. Elana taped decorations to the walls.

E. Elana made a cake.

F. Grandfather said Elana had given him the best gift ever.

Answers: 1. A; 2. B, D, and E; 3. C and F

Conclusions

You and your child come home one day to find piles of clean laundry scattered all over the room. Seeing dog prints on the clothes, you conclude that the dog went through the clothes and made a mess. But your child exclaims, "Oh no! Robots broke into the house and threw all of our clothes around the room!" While this is a creative response that may bring a smile to your face, your child is making a conclusion based on his or her imagination rather than on the evidence at hand.

A child's imagination and creativity can certainly enhance his or her reading experiences. However, they can also be problems when kids start making conclusions about stories based on their own ideas, fantasies, and experiences rather than on the details provided for them by the writer. Good readers know how to make conclusions based on the facts provided for them in the text.

First things first: Get a sense of what your kid already knows. Turn the page and tell your kid to Jump Right In!

Here's what you'll need for this lesson:
- *paper*
- *pencil*
- *index cards*
- *large construction paper or poster board*
- *crayons or markers*

Jump Right In!

Dominos All Around

"Wouldn't it be cool if we could set these up all over the school?" asked Dina. "Sure," Pablo answered. "But how would we do that?" Dina and Pablo were in their classroom. It was their free time. They were setting up dominoes on a table.

"We would need a lot more than 30 dominoes," said Pablo. "Our school has three floors and 30 classrooms!"

Dina said, "It would be funny to see hundreds of tiny rectangles all over the school!" Pablo laughed.

Ms. Green, their teacher, came over. "We're making a domino chain," Pablo told her.

"That looks like fun," said Ms. Green.

"Can we make a domino chain around the school?" Dina asked. "We could ask the kids in our class to help."

"Wow! What a fun idea," said Ms. Green. Pablo and Dina both smiled. "We could make it a math activity," Ms. Green added.

"Yeah," said Pablo. "We can count how many dominoes it will take us. We can even measure it!"

"You can predict how many dominoes it will take," said Ms. Green. The whole class was listening. "We can do it next week during recess," she suggested.

"Great," said Dina. "But who will push the first domino?" she asked. Everyone raised their hand, including Ms. Green!

1. Why do Dina and Pablo need more than 30 dominoes?
   A. to add to their domino collection
   B. to fill up their classroom with dominoes
   C. to use for a math activity
   D. to make a chain around the school

2. Who will help Dina and Pablo?
   A. their parents
   B. their teachers
   C. their classmates
   D. their art teacher

3. Will it be easy to decide who pushes the first domino? Why or why not?

   _____

   _____

4. Does Ms. Green like the idea? What details support your answer?

   _____

   _____

Excellent Job!

 # Checking In

Answers for page 85:

> **1.** D
>
> **2.** C
>
> **3.** An A+ answer: "It will not be easy because everyone wants to push the first domino."
>
> **4.** An A+ answer: "Yes, Ms. Green likes the idea. She says it's a fun idea. She wants to push the first domino."

Did your child get the correct answers? If so, ask how. Make sure your child didn't guess. Tell your child to circle the details that he or she used to find the answers.

Did your child get any of the answers wrong? If so, go over the incorrect answers. Ask, "What made you choose that answer? Where did you find that information in the story?" Check that your child didn't use his or her personal experiences or preferences to answer the questions. Explain that the answers have to be based on the information in the story.

 # Watch Out!

Drawing conclusions is new to second graders. Sometimes, they use their own experiences or preferences to draw conclusions. It's great that they are making connections to the text. But they shouldn't be disregarding the facts in the story in favor of their experiences. If you notice your child misinterpreting details, ask him or her to reread the story and to underline or circle the details.

 # Study Right

Underlining can help your kid focus on details from a passage. Model this for your child by underlining things you need to remember—a train or bus schedule, a grocery list, etc. If you don't need something, draw a line through it. Your child can practice this skill by drawing a line through details that do not support a conclusion or through wrong answer choices.

What to Know...

Kids can use details to draw conclusions about what they're reading.

Review these skills with your child this way:

- A **conclusion** is an idea or thought based on facts.
- **Details** are bits of information in a passage, sometimes given in a word or phrase.
- When you make a conclusion, base it on the details in the passage.

Your child might receive this invitation to a party.

Celebrate Brad's
8th Birthday!

Where: 45 Washington Street
Time: 4:00 p.m.

Bring a bathing suit and
a change of clothes.

Kids should be able to use details to make these conclusions:

- This is a birthday party.
- Kids will be swimming at the party.

 *Checking In*

· · · · · · · · · · · · · · · ·

Ask your child to tell you what type of party this invitation is for. Also, ask who sent the invitation.

Kids shouldn't make conclusions not supported by the given details, such as "It will be a basketball party." Or "Brad's teacher wrote the invitation." If a child gives these answers, he or she may be making conclusions based on his or her personal experiences, preferences, or imagination. Keep directing your child toward the facts in the text, and remind him or her that details support conclusions.

On Your Way to an "A" Activities

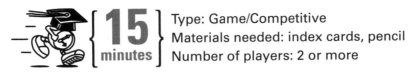

15 minutes

Type: Game/Competitive
Materials needed: index cards, pencil
Number of players: 2 or more

Make and play a memory game. Cut the index cards in half. On one piece, write a detail from the list below. On another piece, write the conclusion that can be drawn from it. Mix up the cards and place them facedown. Take turns turning over two cards. If you get a detail that supports a conclusion, keep the pair. The player with the most cards wins. Add more cards to the game by creating your own details and conclusions.

Detail	Conclusion
There are puddles.	*It's raining outside.*
Jan smiles.	*Jan is happy.*
The Bears scored.	*The Bears won the game.*
There is sauce on our shirts.	*We ate spaghetti.*
The cat meows loudly.	*The cat is hungry.*
John is not in school.	*John is sick.*

Second Graders Are...

Children at this age enjoy explaining their ideas. When your child makes a conclusion, ask for supporting details. Kids' vocabularies are expanding quickly, so the more practice they have with details and conclusions, the faster they can internalize the terms.

Type: Reading/Writing & Arts and Crafts
Materials needed: index cards, large construction paper or poster board, pencils, crayons or markers
Number of players: 1 or more

Make a graphic organizer by connecting details to conclusions. Write each sentence below on a different index card. One of the sentences is the conclusion, while the other three sentences are details. On your paper or poster, glue the conclusion on top, and glue the three details below it. Draw a line connecting the details to the conclusions to show how they are related. Make another graphic organizer using your own sentences.

The table is set.

The turkey is on the table.

It is dinnertime.

We sit at the table.

Type: Game/Competitive
Materials needed: construction paper, scissors, pen
Number of players: 3 or more

Play a version of "20 Questions." Make a crown from a strip of construction paper. One person writes a noun (a person, place, or thing) on the crown. Put the crown on a player so that he or she can't see the word. Take turns giving the player with the crown details about the noun. Write the number of details it takes for the player with the crown to guess the noun. Switch roles. The player with the lowest score wins.

Using Your Head

{20 minutes}

*Grab a **pencil**!*

Look at the picture to figure out where Pablo can find more dominoes in his room.

1. Where should Pablo look for his dominoes?

    A. in his dresser

    B. on his desk

    C. on the rug

    D. next to his magazines

2. Where else should Pablo look for his dominoes?

    A. in one of the boxes

    B. under his pillow

    C. in the bucket of games

    D. on the bookcase

Answers: 1. A; 2. C

Plot and Setting

What happens in this story? Where and when does this story take place? You've probably heard these questions many, many times; you may even remember your own teachers asking them. You probably know that identifying the plot and setting of a story is important and think that it's easy—just find the major events and the location of the story, and you're done. For second graders, however, finding the plot and setting can be tricky.

Plot and setting are new and abstract terms for second graders. Kids may be able to explain what happens in a story, but they may not take care to prioritize the events in a story and may overlook important details. In addition, kids may have trouble differentiating between the setting of a story and the room they're in. To fully understand a story, kids have to understand all of its events in the context of its time and place.

First things first: Get a sense of what your kid already knows. Turn the page and tell your kid to Jump Right In!

Here's what you'll need for this lesson:
- *a fictional story*
- *crayons or markers*
- *construction paper*
- *pencil*

Jump Right In!

Samir's Splash

It was the hottest day of the summer. There were no clouds in the sky. There was no wind. It was a good thing that Samir had just gotten to the public pool in his town. It was early in the morning. He was going to stay at the pool all day.

His friend Jake yelled from the diving board. "Look what I can do!" He ran and jumped up into the water. When he landed, he made a giant splash.

Samir said he could make a big splash too, but Jake said he was too small. Samir walked onto the diving board. He ran and jumped as high as he could. When he landed, water went everywhere! Some water even landed on a lady sitting next to the pool. It was bigger than Jake's splash. Jake said, "Wow!"

1. What sentence from the story helps tell you where Samir is?

    A. He was going to stay at the pool all day.

    B. It was the hottest day of the summer.

    C. Jake said, "Wow!"

    D. There were no clouds in the sky.

2. What time is it in the story?

    A. morning

    B. afternoon

    C. evening

    D. nighttime

3. Write four things that happen in this story.

_____

_____

_____

_____

4. What is the most important event in this story?

_____

_____

_____

_____

Excellent Job!

 *Checking In*

Answers for page 93:

1. A

2. A

3. An A+ answer: "Samir goes to the pool. Jake jumps into the pool. Jake tells Samir that he's too small to jump. Samir jumps into the pool."

4. An A+ answer: "Samir makes a huge splash when he jumps."

Did your child get the correct answers? If so, ask your child to explain how he or she knew what the setting was and what happened in the story. Make sure your child didn't just guess—ask him or her to draw pictures of the setting and what happened in the story.

Did your child get any of the answers wrong? If so, make sure your child understood what each question was asking for. For example, for question 2, ask, "What sentence tells you *when* the story happens?" Though your child may think of the pool as an afternoon destination, it's important that he or she realizes that Samir is there in the morning.

 Watch Out!

When kids are asked to write the events of a story, they often write everything that happens in the story—as many events and details (including the setting) as they can remember. Tell your child to focus on the action of the story—the events that make it up. If his or her version of the events is a little long, it's okay. But if it ends up including almost every detail in the story, help your child decide which are the most important events. Ask him or her to identify the main idea of the story, and then circle or underline the details that relate to that main idea. Learning to discern which details are significant and which are not is an important skill.

What to Know...

Identifying the plot and setting of a story can help your child better understand what he or she is reading.

Review these skills with your child this way:

- The **plot** is the series of events related in a fictional story.

- The **setting** is the time and place in which events in a fictional story take place.

You and your child might read a poem like this:

A Walk Along the River

Along the river we walk
As the sun is shining high,
And the river roars beside us,
Rolling by and by.

Looking down below I see
Water, insects, even plants.
Up above a bird flies by,
And the trees begin to dance.

Jumping in the water quick,
I feel a cool, splashing rush
Of water, leaves, and flowers,
Against me, they all brush.

Ask your child to tell you what is going on in the poem. Then, tell him or her to underline the words that show the setting.

Kids should recognize these events of the plot:

- People walk by a river.

- The speaker runs into the water.

Kids may include that the speaker looks around, but the insects on the ground and the flying bird don't have to be included because they're not important to the main idea of the poem.

Kids should also understand that the setting is a river in the afternoon. Because the poem doesn't explicitly say that it is afternoon, kids have to infer this information from the sun "shining high."

 *Checking In*

If your child missed part of the plot, say, "Let's go back and see what happens in the poem." Try to focus on the big picture rather than on little details. If your child has difficulty with the setting, ask your child to close his or her eyes. Say, "I'm going to read this poem to you while your eyes are closed. Try to picture where and when the actions in this poem are taking place. Pay attention to the sounds, sights, smells, and tastes in the poem." Then, see if she has a better sense of the setting of the poem.

On Your Way to an "A" Activities

30 minutes

Type: Speaking/Listening & Reading/Writing
Materials needed: fictional story
Number of players: 2 or more

Read a story and identify the setting. Then, retell it with a new setting! For example, if you read the book *Nate the Great and the Pillowcase* by Marjorie Sharmat, you can tell the story so it takes place in your neighborhood instead of Nate's. The story can also take place in the afternoon instead of at night. Write down your story and draw pictures for it.

20 minutes

Type: Arts and Crafts
Materials needed: crayons or markers, construction paper
Number of players: 1 or more

Make a back cover for your favorite book. Back covers usually have a picture and a few sentences about the plot of the story. Draw a picture that shows the setting of your favorite book. Then, write a few sentences about the plot, but don't give away the ending!

 *Study Right*

Good readers check comprehension often—help your kid practice this skill by asking him to give you verbal updates as he reads.

Has your child breezed through the activities? If so, he or she can work on this Using Your Head activity independently.

Using Your Head

{ **20** minutes }

*Grab a **pencil**!*

Do you remember these stories?

• "Playing Spaceball on the Moon," page 71

• "The Wind and the Sun," page 60

• "Summer to Fall," page 52

Go back and reread them. Then, fill in the table below with the title, setting, and plot of each story.

Story	Plot	Setting
		The Moon
	The Sun and Wind argue about who is stronger.	
Summer to Fall		

Answers: Row 1: Story: "Playing Spaceball on the Moon." Plot: Felipe is moving to Jupiter. He hopes he can still play spaceball. Setting: The Moon. Row 2: Story: "The Wind and the Sun." Plot: The Sun and Wind argue about who is stronger. They try to get the traveler to take off his jacket. The Sun wins. Setting: Somewhere outside. Row 3: Story: "Summer to Fall." Plot: Dan paints a fall painting after accidentally spilling orange paint. Setting: Dan's house.

Character

Good books bring characters to life, and we come to identify with them as if they were our close friends. Readers of all ages have favorite fictional characters. Finding such a character is one of the most important reading experiences your child can have.

While adults often aspire to be more like the characters they admire, children sometimes expect that characters will be more like them. Kids may answer questions about characters by thinking about themselves. It's great that kids relate to what they're reading. However, good readers know when to focus on the details in the story instead of thinking about themselves and their experiences.

First things first: Get a sense of what your kid already knows. Turn the page and tell your kid to Jump Right In!

Here's what you'll need for this lesson:
- *paper*
- *pencil*
- *a hat*
- *books*

 **Jump Right In!**

Jamie and the Lost Hat

Jamie is always losing things. Last week, she lost her baseball glove. Her father found it in the car later. Jamie also lost a toy. She had left it at a friend's house. Sometimes Jamie finds the things she loses. Sometimes she doesn't.

Jake is Jamie's older brother. He lets Jamie borrow his hats. Jamie is very careful not to lose them. Jake loves his hats. His hats are the only things Jamie has never lost.

One day, Jake wanted to wear his favorite blue hat, but he couldn't find it. "Jamie!" he called. *Oh, no,* thought Jamie. Jake sounded mad. "Where is my blue hat?" he asked. Jamie didn't know. She had worn it yesterday, but she was sure she had returned it. Or had she?

Jamie was nervous. She couldn't remember what she had done with the hat. After all, she was always losing things. Maybe she had meant to put the hat back but had forgotten to do it. That happened often.

Jake was very upset. "You better find it," he said. Jamie searched all over for the hat, but she couldn't find it. What would she do? She had to find that hat!

The next morning, Jamie tripped over the family cat, Patches. She was sleeping outside Jake's room. "Meow!" Patches cried. Then, she ran off, and what did Jamie see on the floor? Jake's blue hat! It was covered with cat hair. Patches had been sleeping on it. Jamie hadn't lost the hat after all.

1. Jamie is a girl who
   A. plays sports
   B. loses things
   C. has lots of hats
   D. borrows toys

2. Jake is Jamie's
   A. twin brother
   B. younger brother
   C. older brother
   D. friend's brother

3. Write two words or phrases that describe Jamie.

   _____

   _____

4. Write two words or phrases that describe Jake.

   _____

   _____

Excellent Job!

 **Checking In**

Ⓐ Answers for page 101:

1. B

2. C

3. An A+ answer: Words and phrases like *forgetful, distracted, careless, loses things, likes hats, likes her brother, likes toys, plays baseball*

4. An A+ answer: Words and phrases like *nice, cares about his things, protective, firm, tough, shares, likes hats, mad*

Did your child get the correct answers? If so, ask your child to underline the parts of the story that led him or her to the answers.

Did your child get any of the answers wrong? If so, ask, "What made you choose that answer?" Kids may focus on what is *possible* instead of what the story says. You can be encouraging but helpful by saying, "That is definitely a possibility" or "That could happen, but we don't know for sure unless the author tells us. Check the passage again."

 **Watch Out!**

Tell your child to underline the words or phrases that describe the characters to make sure that your child is referring to the details in the text and not to his own feelings.

Second Graders Are...

When working with your child, be sure to recognize even the smallest of successes throughout his or her learning. It could be as simple as, "Wow, I like how you read that sentence" or "You really thought about what that character was doing."

What to Know...

When your child reads, he or she meets all kinds of characters. Information about those characters is revealed through details. Understanding characters means sifting through those details to build a picture.

Review this skill with your child this way:

- **Characters** are the people whose actions, ideas, thoughts, and feelings a passage tells us about. Characters aren't always human. Sometimes, animals, plants, or parts of the setting may be characters in a passage. Authors reveal character through details about the character, including what the character says and how the character behaves.

Here's a fun poem about an interesting character.

The Crocodile
By Lewis Carroll

How does the little crocodile
Improve his shining tail,
And pour the waters of the Nile
On every golden scale!

How cheerfully he seems to grin!
How neatly spread his claws,
And welcomes little fishes in
With gently smiling jaws!

. . . .

Ask your child to draw a picture of the character in the poem and to describe him to you.

Good readers might describe the character this way:

- He is a little crocodile with jaws, claws, golden scales, and a shiny tail.

- He grins when he sees fish he is about to eat.

- He swims in the Nile River.

 ## Checking In

Children struggle when they make assumptions that are not supported by details, such as "The crocodile eats humans" or "The crocodile lives in Australia." If a child gives answers like these, she is most likely describing the crocodile based on her own knowledge of fictional or real crocodiles. While making connections with prior knowledge is important, remind your child that when readers describe characters, they get their evidence directly from the text. Explain that this crocodile may be different from the crocodiles your child has seen or read about.

If your child is interested in the fish as characters, that's fine too, but this poem is mainly about the crocodile!

 ## Study Right

Your child may have read a story in which the author seems to be talking directly to him. Explain that some stories have a character who talks directly to us and says things like "I grin cheerfully" or "I spread my claws." Explain to your child that this character is called a *narrator*. Ask your child if he or she has ever read a story or poem in which a narrator was talking or thinking and was part of the story. How does your child feel about the narrator? Is it harder to learn more about that character?

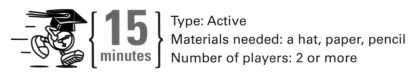

On Your Way to an "A" Activities

{ **15** minutes }

Type: Active
Materials needed: a hat, paper, pencil
Number of players: 2 or more

Play a game of Charades. Write the names of characters from your favorite stories or poems on small pieces of paper. Fold up the papers and put them in a hat. Take turns choosing a name and acting as that character. The other player must guess who you are. The first person to guess correctly wins a point!

{ **20** minutes }

Type: Reading/Writing
Materials needed: book or story, paper, pens
Number of players: 1 or more

Read a story and make a character web. Draw circles on the page, and then write the names of the characters inside the circles. Around the circles, write details about each character from the story. Draw a line connecting the details to the character. See how many details you can come up with for each character.

Has your child breezed through the activities? If so, he or she can work on this Using Your Head activity independently.

Using Your Head

*Grab a **pencil**!*

Look at the picture of Patches below. Write a description of Patches. Write at least 5 details.

Answers: Sample description: Patches is gray and striped. She is playful and friendly. She likes to play with hats. She is happy. She is hungry.

Putting Events in Order

Second graders usually live very structured lives; at school and at home they're constantly being told what to do, how to do it, and when to do it. So when they are asked to figure out the order of something—like the sequence of events in a passage—they often struggle. This is especially true when authors include events out of order and expect readers to figure out the order in which they occurred.

Good readers think about the sequence of events while reading. Putting events in order helps a reader organize a story in his or her mind. Paying attention to the sequence of events in a story or passage can help your kid understand what she or he is reading and help her or him to summarize the text.

First things first: Get a sense of what your kid already knows. Turn the page and tell your kid to Jump Right In!

Here's what you'll need for this lesson:

- index cards
- beach ball
- construction paper
- glue or tape
- glitter
- yarn
- paper
- pencil
- scissors
- timer
- books or stories

Jump Right In!

Lanterns for the New Year

My name is Lisa. Last week, my friend Ling invited me over. She was celebrating Chinese New Year. Chinese New Year is also called the Spring Festival. It is the oldest holiday in China.

Ling's mom asked us to make decorations. "Let's make lanterns for the Lantern Festival," Ling said. A lantern is a lamp that people carry on the streets.

Ling and I had fun making lanterns. First, we folded a piece of construction paper in half the long way. Then, we cut lines along the folded part of the paper. We did not cut the lines all the way through. Next, we unfolded the paper and glued the edges together. Then, we cut a strip of paper for the handle. We glued it in two places on top of the lantern. We added glitter to make the lanterns shiny!

We made lots of lanterns in different colors. Ling suggested that we hang them up with yarn. We hung the lanterns up in the kitchen. They looked great. I went home and made some lanterns for my room!

1. What happened *first* in the story?

   A. Ling and Lisa decided to make lanterns.

   B. Ling and Lisa folded construction paper.

   C. Ling's mom asked them to make cookies.

   D. Ling's mom asked them to make decorations.

2. What did Ling and Lisa do *before* they cut lines in the paper?

   A. They folded the paper.

   B. They glued the sides together.

   C. They cut a strip of paper for the handle.

   D. They glued the handle to the lantern.

3. What did the girls do *after* they glued the sides together?

   _____

   _____

   _____

4. What happened at the end of the story?

   _____

   _____

   _____

Excellent Job!

 **Checking In**

Answers for page 109:

1. D

2. A

3. An A+ answer: "They cut a piece of paper and glued it on top for the handle."

4. An A+ answer: "Lisa went home and made lanterns for her room."

Did your child get the correct answers? If so, ask your child how she found the answers. Make sure your child didn't guess. Ask her how she figured out the sequence of events. Did she number the steps?

Did your child get any of the answers wrong? If so, ask your child to retell the events of the story. Model the skill by beginning, "First, Lisa went to Ling's house. Then, Ling's mom asked them to make decorations. What happened next?" Keep asking your child what happened next until you reach the end of the story. Have your child write each event down and number them in the order that they happened.

 **Watch Out!**

If your child mixed up the sequence of events, ask specific questions about what would happen if the events were out of order. For example, in question 3, if your child wrote that Lisa and Ling hung the lanterns on a string after gluing the sides together, you might ask your child to draw a picture of a lantern and then point to the handle and ask, "What part is this?" Help your child to recognize that the handle was put on after the sides were glued but before the lanterns were hung.

Second Graders Are...

Second graders really like structure in their lives. Structure gives them a sense of security in a world that's constantly changing. When children understand the structure of something, such as their daily schedule, they are more relaxed and they are better able to complete tasks. For these reasons, students usually enjoy sequencing activities. When children see the structure of a story, they find it easier to make summaries, predictions, connections, and conclusions; to notice details about the characters, plot, and setting; and to develop higher-order thinking skills, such as using the information in the text to generate new ideas.

What to Know...

Kids need to pay close attention to the sequence of events because texts may not always list events in the order they happen.

Review this skill with your child this way:

- **Sequence** is the order of ideas and events in a passage. The sequence in which events are presented in a passage may or may not be the same as the order in which the events described actually took place.
- Children can describe sequence using the words *before* and *after*.

Read this passage with your child.

> Hannah is in the middle of drawing a picture of her favorite animals. Yesterday, Hannah went to the zoo. She saw tigers and lions and elephants at the zoo. Then, she saw baby seals swimming in the water. Now, she is asking her parents to take her there again. Her parents promise to take her next week.

Good readers use key words, such as *yesterday* and *now,* to put the events in the order in which they happened:

- Yesterday, Hannah went to the zoo.
- She saw tigers and lions and elephants at the zoo.
- Then, she saw baby seals swimming in the water.
- Hannah is in the middle of drawing a picture of her favorite animals.
- Now, she is asking her parents to take her there again.
- Her parents promise to take her next week.

· · · · · · · · · · · · · ·

Ask your child to tell you the order of the events in the passage. Tell your child to circle the words that helped him or her figure out the order.

 *Study Right*

In addition to *now* and *yesterday,* other key words that can help your child put events in order include *before, after, first, second, third, then, next,* and *finally.* Encourage your child to circle or underline these words as he or she reads.

On Your Way to an "A" Activities

20 minutes

Type: Active
Materials needed: four index cards, tape, beach ball, a book or a passage from this book
Number of players: 2 or more

On each index card, write one of these words: *beginning*, *middle*, *end*, or *whole story*. Tape the cards to a beach ball. Read a book or a passage from this book together. Take turns tossing the ball. Whatever section is facing you, tell what happened at that part of the story. For example, if you get *middle*, tell any event that happened in the middle of the story. If you get *whole story*, tell all the events in the story in order. Do this with several passages or stories.

15 minutes

Type: Arts and Crafts
Materials needed: paper, construction paper, glue or tape, scissors, yarn, glitter
Number of players: 1 or more

First, list each step that Lisa and Ling took to make lanterns in the story "Lanterns for the New Year." Then, follow these steps to make your own lanterns.

Type: Game/Competitive
Materials needed: paper, pencil, scissors, story, timer
Number of players: 1 or more

Play "Mixed-Up Message to Mars." Imagine that you want to send a message to Mars. You are going to tell aliens all about an activity that you do every day. On a piece of paper, write the steps you take for activities you do every day, such as tying your shoes or eating breakfast. Make sure to write each step as a separate sentence. Give each step a lot of space on the paper. Now, cut out each step as a strip of paper. Mix up the strips, and give them to your partner. Pretend that somehow your message to Mars got mixed up. Your partner should pretend to be an alien and figure out the correct message. Time your partner to see how long it takes to arrange the events in the correct order. Challenge yourself by mixing up steps to many activities at the same time. Now, have your partner write steps on paper and mix them up, and you can pretend to be the alien trying to figure out the message!

Has your child breezed through the activities? If so, he or she can work on this Using Your Head activity independently.

Using Your Head

{ **5** minutes }

*Grab a **pencil**!*

Lisa and Ling did another project together. Number the steps they took so the steps are in the right order.

_____ They drew the outline of dragons.

_____ They put the brushes and paints away.

_____ Lisa and Ling decided to make dragon paintings.

_____ They hung their paintings on the wall.

_____ Lisa and Ling added color to the dragons.

_____ They set up their paints.

Answers: 3, 5, 1, 6, 4, 2

Problem and Solution

Most stories center around a problem that needs to be solved. Identifying that problem and its solution is an important comprehension skill for children to learn. However, second graders may have trouble finding problems and solutions because they end up focusing on their own likes and dislikes instead of focusing on the details in the passage.

For example, your child might read about Jimmy, a hungry fellow, sitting down to eat fish and green beans for dinner. Just as Jimmy grabs his fork, Fluffy, his equally hungry dog, jumps up and gobbles down all the food! You probably think that the problem in this story is obvious—Fluffy ate all the food and left nothing for Jimmy! However, if your child hates fish and green beans, he or she might say that the problem is that poor Jimmy was forced to eat fish and green beans—a form of cruel punishment in your child's mind. To correctly identify the problem and its solution, your child needs to focus only on the information in the passage and shouldn't let his or her likes and dislikes interfere.

First things first: Get a sense of what your kid already knows. Turn the page and tell your kid to Jump Right In!

Here's what you'll need for this lesson:
- paper
- markers
- pencil
- construction paper

Jump Right In!

Our Flying Friend

It was a beautiful spring Saturday. Jacob and I were playing Frisbee in the park. Our dads are friends. Sometimes, the four of us come to the park. Our dads like to sit on the benches and talk. We like to play Frisbee.

"Throw me a long one," I said. Jacob took a hop and threw the Frisbee. It looked so cool spinning around, but it was going over my head! I tried to run back, but it was too far. I walked to where the Frisbee landed. There was a cute bird next to it. "What are you looking at, Sarah?" Jacob yelled.

"There's a little bird here," I answered. Our dads came over. "It looks like its wing might be hurt," I told them. The bird was trying to fly, but it could not. "What should we do?" I asked my dad. "Let's tell the police officer over there," he said.

We told the police officer. She said, "There is a special hospital for birds. They will take care of it." She gave us the phone number. We called the number. Someone from the hospital came and took the bird away. The next week we got a call from the bird hospital. The bird was okay! As soon as the bird can fly, the animal doctor will let it out in the park. She said we can watch!

1. What is the biggest problem in this story?

   A. Sarah doesn't catch the Frisbee.

   B. Sarah finds a hurt bird.

   C. Jacob throws the Frisbee too far.

   D. Jacob finds a hurt squirrel.

2. How did the characters solve their problem?

   A. They brought the bird to a bird hospital.

   B. They asked a police officer for help.

   C. They looked all over the park for the Frisbee.

   D. They kept the bird as a pet and took care of it.

3. What did the police officer say to do?

   _____

   _____

   _____

4. How would you have solved the problem?

   _____

   _____

   _____

Excellent Job!

Checking In

Answers for page 117:

1. B

2. B

3. An A+ answer: "The police officer gave them a phone number for a bird hospital."

4. An A+ answer: "I would have taken care of the bird."

Did your child get the correct answers? If so, check that your kid wasn't just guessing. Ask your child how he or she identified the problem and the solution. Ask if the passage included more than one problem and solution.

Did your child get any of the answers wrong? If your child chose another answer for question 1, ask if that answer choice was really the biggest problem in this story. Your kid may pick a problem that did happen in the story but something that wasn't the biggest problem. If this happens, ask your child to locate every problem in the story. Then, he or she should pick the problem that the passage focused on the most.

Watch Out!

Second graders may have trouble finding the solutions to story problems. When asked to identify the solution in the story, they may automatically give the solution that they would use if they were in the story. Remind your child that his or her answers always need to come from the story and need to be supported by details. Asking kids to underline or circle the solution in the passage will help them remember to use only the details in the text to decide an answer.

What to Know...

Identifying the main problem in a story—and its solution—involves being able to critically evaluate information and sort out the most important parts.

Review this skill with your child this way:

- A **problem** in a passage may be between a character and another character, between a character and society, between a character and nature, or between a character and himself or herself. Sometimes there is a problem between opposing groups of characters.

Your child may be able to relate to Diego's problem in this passage.

Diego forgot to bring a ball for recess. He asked a teacher if he could get a ball from the gym. His teacher said, "Okay." When Diego got to the gym, he noticed that there was a class going on. Kids were sitting down listening to the teacher. So, Diego waited to ask for a ball.

Ask your child what Diego's problem is.

Kids might identify the problem as:

- Diego forgot his ball.

- Diego wanted to get a ball from the gym, but there was a class going on.

Both answers are right. You could view this short passage as having two separate problems. Diego solved the first problem by asking his teacher if he could get another ball. But, as he tried to solve his first problem, he encountered another problem.

Kids might notice the following solutions:

- Diego tried to solve the problem of forgetting the ball by asking for one.

- Diego tried to solve the problem of there being a class in the gym by waiting to ask to borrow the ball.

On Your Way to an "A" Activities

{ **20** minutes }

Type: Reading/Writing
Materials needed: paper, pencil
Number of players: 2 or more

Write your own story! Think of a problem your character or characters will face in the story, then discuss with your partner how to solve it. Make a list of at least three possible solutions before you write the story. What makes each solution different? Which one do you like the best? Now, work together to write what happens.

{ **20** minutes }

Type: Active
Materials needed: story
Number of players: 2 or more

Act out the story you've written. Before you get to the end, see if your audience can guess what happens next.

Type: Reading/Writing
Materials needed: paper, pencil
Number of players: 1 or more

Think of a book you enjoy or a movie you like. How many problems can you think of from that book or movie? Brainstorm alone or with another person to list as many as you can. Now, can you think of how all those problems were solved? Make a list to show the problems in one column and the solutions in another. If there are problems that were not solved, write what you think should happen to solve them!

Second Graders Are...

Reading about a character's problems and solutions in a story can be an important learning experience for kids. It's sometimes easier to think about and solve a character's problems than your own. There are many children's books that deal with real issues that young kids face—friendship issues, safety issues, divorce, and death. Reading a story about a character who is feeling something similar to what a child is feeling can help him work through his own problem.

Using Your Head

[**10** minutes]

*Grab a **pencil**!*

Read the story below. Answer the questions that follow.

A rabbit was hopping home from town. He was carrying a pie from the bakery. He lived two miles from town. He was already late for dinner. The rabbit felt raindrops on his nose. A minute later, it began to pour. The pie got very wet and started dripping. He tried to clean it up, but it fell apart. When the rabbit looked up, he couldn't see the road. The rain had washed his trail away! He was lost. He hopped around for an hour. Finally, he just sat down and cried. All of a sudden, he heard his name. His family came looking for him and found him. "I'm sorry I'm late and I ruined the pie," he said. "That's okay," said his sister. "We don't care about the pie. We just want you home with us!" The rabbit family hopped happily home in the rain.

What is the biggest problem in this story?

_____

_____

How was this problem solved?

_____

_____

Answers: Problem: The rabbit was lost and wanted to go home. Solution: His family found him.

Comparing and Contrasting

Second graders are starting to read more complex texts, with more and more details, characters, and settings. As the amount of information they get from a text grows, kids can become overwhelmed. How are they ever going to keep all of this straight in their heads?

Luckily, there is help: notes, lists, and Venn diagrams can help readers easily compare and contrast different things. Practice also helps—kids need to practice retaining information and locating important details. The ability to compare and contrast is strongly tied to reading comprehension and general understanding.

First things first: Get a sense of what your kid already knows. Turn the page and tell your kid to Jump Right In!

Here's what you'll need for this lesson:
- *fruits and vegetables*
- *two of your favorite books*
- *two friends or relatives*
- *pencil*
- *blindfold*

 **Jump Right In!**

The Holly and the Elm

The American holly tree and the American elm tree are both common trees. You can find them in many places. They grow as far south as Texas. They grow as far north as Massachusetts. The American elm is even more common than the American holly tree. The elm usually lives in the middle of the United States. That is far from the coast. The holly lives only close to the coast.

Both trees are beautiful. Elm trees are taller, though. They can grow up to 100 feet tall. Holly trees grow up to 70 feet tall.

Elm and holly trees both have green leaves, but in the fall, elm leaves change. They turn yellow. Then they fall off. That does not happen to the holly. Its leaves stay the same all year. Holly leaves are very sharp.

Holly leaf   **Elm leaf**

Cracking the Second Grade

1. What is one way that the American elm tree and the American holly tree are alike?

   A. They both have sharp leaves.

   B. They both have green leaves.

   C. They both can grow to 100 feet tall.

   D. The leaves of both fall off in the fall.

2. What is one way that the American elm tree and the American holly tree are different?

   A. The elm's leaves turn yellow.

   B. The American holly tree is beautiful.

   C. They are both common trees.

   D. Neither tree lives in Nevada.

3. How are the locations of the American elm tree and the American holly tree alike? How are their locations different?

   _____

   _____

   _____

4. Look at the pictures of the leaves. Write one way that they are alike. Write one way that they are different.

   _____

   _____

   _____

Excellent Job!

 ## Checking In

ⒶAnswers for page 125:

1. B

2. A

3. An A+ answer: "Both the elm and holly trees grow from Texas to Massachusetts, but the elm grows in the middle of the United States. The holly grows only closer to the coast."

4. An A+ answer: "Both leaves have a line down the middle. The holly leaf has sharper edges."

Did your child get the correct answers? If so, ask your child to explain how he or she knew the differences and similarities. Ask your child to tell you where he or she found the information.

Did your child get any of the answers wrong? If so, go over the incorrect answers. If your child had trouble finding similarities, point out that the statement must be true for both trees. If your child had trouble finding differences, point out that the statement must be true for only one of the two trees. (If it is true for *neither* tree, then it is another way that they are alike!) For each detail, ask your child, "Is this true for both trees or only one tree?"

 ## Watch Out!

Kids may have trouble remembering which detail goes with which tree. Remind your child that he or she can always go back to the passage to review the words. Encourage your child to make a list and to put all the details about the holly tree in one column and to put all the details about the elm tree in another column. A list makes it easy to see which details match and which details don't match.

What to Know...

Kids often mix up the meanings of the words *comparing* and *contrasting*.

Review these skills with your child this way:

- **Comparing** is noting what is alike between two or more ideas, characters, details, or events in a passage.

- **Contrasting** is noting what is different between two or more ideas, characters, details, or events in a passage.

- Children can use the words *alike* and *different*.

Your child can practice comparing and contrasting with the passage below.

Mouse and Bear are best friends. They like to play the same games. They both live in the forest. They eat the same food, but Bear eats a lot more. He is huge. Mouse is tiny.

One day, a big storm came. It rained and rained. The white fur on Mouse and the brown fur on Bear got wet. Bear was scared, but Mouse said, "Don't be scared. It will stop raining. Then, it will be sunny again!" Bear smiled. He knew Mouse was right. Mouse was very smart, and Bear was glad that Mouse was very brave too!

· · · · · · · · · · · · · ·

Ask your child to compare Mouse and Bear by drawing a picture of them and then writing words that describe each animal. Ask, "What do they look like? How do they act? What words describe them?"

Kids should recognize these similarities between Mouse and Bear:

- They play the same games.

- They live in the forest.

- They eat the same food.

- Their fur gets wet.

Kids should also recognize these differences between Mouse and Bear:

- Bear eats more food.

- Bear is big. Mouse is small.

- Bear has brown fur. Mouse has white fur.

- Bear is scared. Mouse is brave and smart.

Kids struggle when they compare or contrast without using the details provided in the passage. For example, they may say that Mouse has a pink nose and Bear has a black nose because they are thinking of pictures of animals. Remind your kid to stay true to the words in the passage when comparing and contrasting.

Watch Out!

Help kids keep the words *compare* and *contrast* straight by using mnemonics such as *compare* has an "m" so it means that things *match,* and *contrast* has an "n" so it means that things do *not*.

Giving your kid more practice with topics that he knows well will also help him become more familiar with the terms. Ask your child to compare and contrast siblings, pets, seasons, or anything else familiar.

Second Graders Are...

Second graders are starting to reflect and to become more aware of their own circumstances as opposed to the circumstances of the characters in books. When they read about characters, they can pause to consider the differences between characters, or between themselves and the characters.

On Your Way to an "A" Activities

 10 *minutes* Type: Game/Competitive
Materials needed: fruits, vegetables, a blindfold
Number of players: 2 or more

One player should be blindfolded. Then, this player has to take a bite out of different fruits and vegetables. This player identifies how the fruits and vegetables are alike and how they are different (taste, touch, or smell). Then, this player takes off the blindfold. Go over what the player noticed. Then, take turns. After every player has had a chance to taste the fruit and vegetables with the blindfold on, talk together about how the fruits and vegetables are alike and how they are different. Which ones are most alike? Which are least alike?

15 *minutes* Type: Speaking/Listening
Materials needed: two friends or relatives
Number of players: 3 or more

Bring two friends or relatives into a room. Tell them three ways that they are the same. You could say, "You both have long hair" or "You both are very smart." Then, tell them three ways that they are different.

 *Study Right*

Remind your child that comparing and contrasting doesn't have to be something that he does when he's finished a story. It can be something that he is considering *throughout* the story.

Using Your Head

{10 minutes}

*Grab a **pencil**!*

Reread "The Story of Rosa Parks" on page 76 and "Fly to the Moon" on page 68. Then, compare and contrast the passages. Write the number of each sentence under "Rosa Parks," "Neil Armstrong," or "Both" in the Venn diagram.

1. Lived in the 1900s
2. Refused to give up a seat on a bus
3. Hero to many people
4. Story set in American south
5. Story set in outer space
6. Did something important
7. Walked on the Moon
8. Was very brave
9. Was a woman

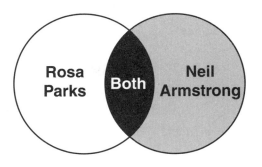

Answers: Both: Lived in 1900s, Hero to many people, Did something important, Was very brave. Rosa Parks: Refused to give up a seat on a bus, Was a woman, Story set in American south. Neil Armstrong: Story set in outer space, Walked on the Moon

Cause and Effect

Effects in life and in stories have causes. Sometimes, the cause of an effect is obvious—a person gets wet (effect) because it rains (cause). Sometimes the cause is implied—Gary orders a pizza for dinner (effect) because, *we assume,* he is hungry (cause).

Cause-and-effect relationships can be tricky for second graders. As second graders develop their reading comprehension skills, they are beginning to read longer and more involved stories and books. Young readers are sometimes more focused on the events of a story than the relationships between the events. This is especially problematic when the cause of an event is not directly stated or when the cause of an event is realized later on in a story. Good readers read carefully and know that sometimes causes aren't always spelled out.

First things first: Get a sense of what your kid already knows. Turn the page and tell your kid to Jump Right In!

Here's what you'll need for this lesson:
- a book
- two different-colored highlighters
- a pencil
- paper
- index cards

Jump Right In!

Hot Air Balloons

How did people first fly in the air? Did they use an airplane? Nope. They used a hot air balloon! People first flew in a balloon in 1783. Two men rode in the balloon. They started in Paris. The balloon stayed in the air for 25 minutes. It got as far as 100 meters above the ground.

Many people love to ride in hot air balloons. Riding in a balloon can be fun and calming. People can see for miles and miles. Houses look like toys because they are so tiny. People do not feel wind when they are riding. The balloon moves with the wind. People feel wind only if the balloon goes up or down.

People today have fun with hot air balloons. Some even have races with balloons. Their balloons can come in many colors. Balloons can have different shapes too. Some look like hot dogs. Other balloons look like rocket ships. What shape balloon would you like?

Balloons that carry people have a gas bag and a basket. The bag is what most people call the balloon. People ride in the basket. What lifts the balloon? A burner sits under the gas bag. It warms the air in the bag. Warm air is lighter than cold air. So, the warm air in the bag makes the balloon rise!

1. People do not feel wind in a hot air balloon because

    A. the air is always very hot

    B. there is very little wind

    C. the balloon moves with the wind

    D. the balloon flies only on clear days

2. Warm air inside makes the balloon

    A. go down

    B. go up

    C. move side to side

    D. blow up

3. In a hot air balloon, people see for many miles because

_____

_____

4. Why do the houses look like toys, as mentioned in paragraph 2?

_____

_____

Excellent Job!

 **Checking In**

Answers for page 133:

1. C

2. B

3. An A+ answer: "They are high above the ground."

4. An A+ answer: "When you are far away from things, they look smaller."

Did your child get the correct answers? If so, ask how. Ask your child to explain the cause and effect by saying, "If _____ happens, then _____ happens."

Did your child get any of the answers wrong? If so, go over the incorrect answers. Rephrase each question as a cause-and-effect relationship. For example, ask your child to reread the story to find out what causes people not to feel wind or what effect warm air has on a balloon. If necessary, explain the difference between a *cause* and an *effect*: A cause is the reason an event happens. An effect is the result of an event, feeling, or idea.

 **Watch Out!**

Identifying cause and effect can be tricky when cause-and-effect relationships aren't presented explicitly. To answer questions 3 and 4, your child needs to make inferences. If your child got question 3 wrong, tell him or her that the author sometimes leaves details out. The answer to this question isn't in the passage, so a reader must imagine what causes a person to see for miles and miles. If your child has been in an airplane, on a mountain, or in a tall building, remind him or her of that experience. Ask your child, "When you're in a hot air balloon, you're very high up. Think of a time when you were high up (like in an airplane). Could you see for miles and miles? Why?"

Question 4 also asks about an implied cause-and-effect relationship. If your child had difficulties with that question, remind him or her again of being high up or far away from something. Make a game of examining perspective by asking your child to make a viewfinder by forming her thumbs and index fingers into a square. What can she see through her viewfinder when she is 3 feet from an object? 10 feet? 20 feet? More?

What to Know...

Kids can struggle with cause-and-effect relationships, especially when they are not stated explicitly in a text.

Review these skills with your child this way:

- The **cause** is the reason an event happens.
- The **effect** is the result of an event, feeling, or idea.

Below are two cause-and-effect relationships that you and your child might see in a story.

1. "Ben, we're going to California to visit your cousins next week," Dad said. Ben was happy.

2. Ben is very happy. He just found out that his family is going on a trip to California to visit his cousins.

Ask your child what the cause and effect are in each sentence. Ask your child to tell you how the sentences are alike and how they are different.

Kids should understand that the cause-and-effect relationship is the same in both examples. The cause is Ben and his family going to California. The effect is Ben being happy. The author just changed the order.

 *Checking In*

Kids may struggle because they assume that the first sentence is always the cause. If this happens to your child, help him or her to understand the logic of the example to determine which sentence could have caused which sentence. Ask, "Did Ben's family plan a trip to California because Ben was happy? Or did Ben become happy when he found out that his family was going to California?" Explain that the cause always happens before the effect, but the writer doesn't have to mention the cause first.

On Your Way to an "A" Activities

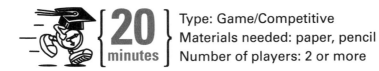

Type: Game/Competitive
Materials needed: paper, pencil
Number of players: 2 or more

Play "Cause-and-Effect Tic-Tac-Toe." Set up the game by making a big tic-tac-toe board on a piece of paper. Do this by drawing two lines up and down. Then, draw two lines from left to right across your earlier lines. This will make nine equal spaces. Next, write a cause in each square. Leave space in the square. The other player must write a matching effect underneath it before he or she can write an *X* or an *O* in the square. For the next game, write an effect in the square. Players must then write a possible cause in order to win that space.

Below are some examples you can use. Think of five more causes and effects. They can be real or from a story.

Causes: I took a bath, I was hungry, my shoes were untied, I looked at my watch.

Effects: I became clean, I got an apple, I tripped on my shoelaces, I noticed I was late.

 *Study Right*

The words *if* and *then* are helpful to use when learning about cause and effect. *If* goes with the cause and *then* goes with the effect, as in the example, *"If* I walk close to the surf, *then* my feet will get wet." Guide your child to use these words with cause-and-effect relationships.

Type: Reading/Writing
Materials needed: a book, two different-colored highlighters, pencil
Number of players: 1 or more

Pick a book you can write in, or a passage from this book. Read a story and pay attention to the events and to the feelings and ideas the characters have. Highlight the causes in one color and the effects in the other. If an event is missing a cause or effect, write it in the margin of the story.

Type: Game/Competitive
Materials needed: paper, pencil, index cards
Number of players: 2 or more

Play a memory game with cause and effect. Cut index cards in half. On one half, write a cause. On the other half, write its effect. Mix up the cards and place them facedown. Players take turns choosing two cards and looking for a match. The player with the most matches wins.

Here are some cause-and-effect examples to get you started:

If I pedal my bike, then it will move.

If I stay up too late, then I will be tired.

If I eat a healthy breakfast, then I will have energy.

If I read a lot, then I will become a good reader.

Has your child breezed through the activities? If so, he or she can work on this Using Your Head activity independently.

Using Your Head

{ **5** minutes }

*Grab a **pencil**!*

Fill in the causes or effects.

Causes	Effects
1. I jumped in the pool.	_____
2. _____	I laughed.
3. _____	I was hot.
4. Sal mixed paints.	_____
5. Jim watered the plants.	_____

Answers: 1. I made a big splash. 2. I read a joke. 3. The sun was shining. 4. Sal made a new color. 5. The plants grew.

Place Value

Kids are very visual creatures. They can have trouble understanding something if they can't see it in front of them. Large numbers, for example, can be confusing because they're hard to visualize. It's easy for your kid to understand the number 12 because he or she has 12 socks in a drawer or has painted 12 pictures for school. However, a number like 4,312 is more difficult because he or she hasn't held 4,312 of anything.

If your child doesn't understand the place value of 4,312, then he or she may think that 4,312 and 1,423 mean the same thing because they use the same digits. Place value can help your child understand that 4,312 means 4 thousands, 3 hundreds, 1 ten, and 2 ones. Visual aids, such as base-ten blocks and place-value charts, can help your child grasp the place value of each digit and understand what large numbers really mean.

First things first: Get a sense of what your kid already knows. Turn the page and tell your kid to Jump Right In!

Here's what you'll need for this lesson:

- *timer*
- *poster board*
- *crayons or markers*
- *index cards*
- *6 paper cups*
- *a large amount of beans or cereal*
- *glue*

Jump Right In!

1. The largest known polar bear weighed 2,210 pounds. What is the place value of 1 in this number?

    A. thousands

    B. hundreds

    C. tens

    D. ones

2. What number does this group of base-ten blocks show?

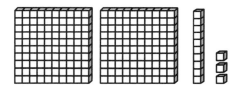

    A. 123

    B. 213

    C. 231

    D. 312

3. The Empire State Building has 1,860 steps. What digit is in the thousands place in this number?

    A. 1

    B. 8

    C. 6

    D. 0

4. What number does this place-value chart show?

hundreds	tens	ones
3	0	2

    A. 202

    B. 232

    C. 302

    D. 320

5. Write the number that has

    7 in the tens place

    2 in the hundreds place

    4 in the ones place

    1 in the thousands place

6. Some dinosaurs were 130 feet long. Draw base-ten blocks to show the number 130.

Excellent Job!

 *Checking In*

Answers for pages 142 and 143:

1. C

2. B

3. A

4. C

5. An A+ answer: 1,274

6. An A+ answer: One flat and 3 rods should be drawn.

Did your child get the correct answers? If so, ask how. You could say, "How did you find the place value of the digit? Did you think of a place-value chart or use base-ten blocks?" Ask your child for the place value of each digit in questions 1 and 3. For question 1, for example, ask, "What is the place value of 0? What is the place value of 1? What is the place value of each 2?"

Did your child get any of the answers wrong? If so, go over the incorrect answers. Ask, "What did you do to find your answer?" For questions 2 and 4, ask students to name the value of each base-ten block and the value of each column in the place-value chart. Help your child understand the relationship between base-ten blocks and place-value charts. Ask which block belongs in the ones column and confirm that your kid knows it is the unit block. Then, ask which block belongs in the tens column and confirm that your kid knows it is the rod. Do the same with the hundreds column and the flat.

 *Watch Out!*

Second graders might have trouble remembering when and where to place a comma in a number. Tell your child to find and circle the commas in questions 1 and 3. Explain that the comma separates the hundreds from the thousands. Encourage your child to write a comma between the hundreds and thousands columns in place-value charts.

 *Study Right*

Though it is commonplace to say "twenty-two ten" or "eighteen-sixty" for the numbers 2,210 and 1,860, make sure your child practices saying the number's actual value: "Two thousand two hundred ten." This will help him focus on place value.

What to Know...

Every number your child encounters—in school or at home—has place value.
Review this skill with your child this way:

- A **digit** is a symbol that is used to write numbers. There are 10 digits: 0, 1, 2, 3, 4, 5, 6, 7, 8, and 9.

- **Place value** is the value of a digit based on its place in a number. For example, in the number 382, the digit 8 is in the tens place, so it has a value of 80.

In school, kids generally learn place value by using these base-ten blocks.

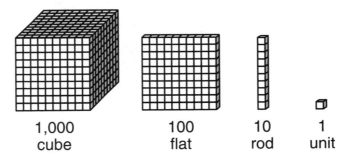

| 1,000 cube | 100 flat | 10 rod | 1 unit |

Your child can use place value to read prices.

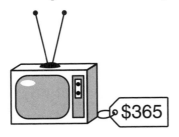

$365

· · · · · · · · · · · · ·

Ask your child to say the digits in the number 365. Then, ask your child for the value of each digit.

 *Checking In*

The digits in the price are 3, 6, and 5. However, their values aren't 3, 6, and 5. Ask your child what the 3 shows. Help your child see that because 3 is in the hundreds place, it has a value of 300, not 3 or 30. Ask your child for the value of the 6 and 5, and make sure that he or she understands that the values of the digits are 60 and 5. To help your child understand the value of each digit, have him or her count out beans in groups of 300, 60, and 5. Then, ask him or her to compare these groups with groups of 3, 6, and 5 beans. Check that your child understands the difference between 300 beans and 3 beans and between 60 beans and 6 beans by asking him or her to write how many are in each group.

On Your Way to an "A" Activities

Type: Game/Competitive & Arts and Crafts
Materials needed: timer, poster board, crayons or markers
Number of players: 2 or more

Each player will go on a 10-minute scavenger hunt to find the largest three-digit number in the house. Ask a grown-up to keep the time. Look for numbers in the phone book, on store fliers or pieces of mail, and anywhere else you can think of. When time is called, write the largest number you found using words, a place-value chart, and base-ten blocks on a poster board. Use different colors to show each place value. Then, show your number. The player with the largest number wins!

Type: Reading/Writing
Materials needed: poster board, crayons or markers
Number of players: 1 or more

Copy the poem below on poster board to help you remember place value order from ones to thousands.

As you read from left to right,

the values go from big to slight:

thousand and hundred, but you're not done,

here is the ten and there is the one.

Recite the poem to family members. Then, hang your writing or drawing somewhere you'll see it every day!

Type: Speaking/Listening & Game/Competitive
Materials needed: none
Number of players: 2

Say any three digits. The other player will then say the number using place value. For example, if you say "three, zero, four," the other player should say, "Three hundreds, zero tens, and four ones." The player wins a point if he or she is correct. The first player to reach 10 points wins.

Type: Game/Competitive
Materials needed: 20 index cards, a pencil
Number of players: 3 or more

Play the game "300." Ask your parent or another grown-up to write numbers with four or five digits on index cards. Tell the grown-up to show you and the other players the cards one at a time. If the number has the digit 3 in the hundreds place, clap your hands. The first player to clap gets a point. If the number does not have a 3 in the hundreds place, stay silent. If a player claps for the wrong number, he or she loses a point. The first player to get 5 points wins.

Second Graders Are...

Second graders are often perfectionists and are easily frustrated by the pressures of time. The time frames given for each activity are estimates. Give your child more time if he or she needs it.

Has your child breezed through the activities? If so, he or she can work on this Using Your Head activity independently.

Using Your Head

{ **25** minutes }

*Grab **6 paper cups**, lots of **beans**, a **pencil**, a **poster**, and some **glue**!*

Write one of these labels on each cup: ones, tens, hundreds, thousands, ten thousands, hundred thousands.

Fill the cups with beans to show the numbers below.

1,324
57,809
841,010
6,739

Put the number of ones in the ones cup, the number of tens in the tens cup, and so on.

Draw a place-value chart (like the one at the beginning of the lesson) on your poster. Include columns up to hundred thousands. After finishing each number, glue the right number of beans into the place-value chart.

Answers: 1,324: 1 thousand, 3 hundreds, 2 tens, 4 ones; **57,809:** 5 ten thousands, 7 thousands, 8 hundreds, 0 tens, 9 ones; **841,010:** 8 hundred thousands, 4 ten thousands, 1 thousand, 0 hundreds, 1 ten, 0 ones; **6,739:** 6 thousands, 7 hundreds, 3 tens, 9 ones

Addition

Just like other second graders, yours is probably eager to please. Your kid may be excited to explore the concept of addition, but she might not always do her math correctly. You want to encourage your child to keep learning and to approach math with confidence, yet you also want your child to really understand what she is doing.

For example, you may notice that your kid has to add 23 and 19 for homework and is struggling with regrouping. She knows that 3 plus 9 equals 12, but she might not be sure where to write these numbers. She might write "12" and then move on to add 2 and 1 to get 3, for a final answer of 312 instead of 42. To get the correct answer, your kid should rewrite 12 ones as 1 ten and 2 ones and then add the numbers in the tens columns. Regrouping can be tough, but you can help your child understand the concept.

First things first: Get a sense of what your kid already knows. Turn the page and tell your kid to Jump Right In!

Here's what you'll need for this lesson:
- *O-shaped cereal or pennies*
- *deck of cards*
- *paper*
- *crayons or markers*
- *pencil*
- *dice*
- *poster board*
- *stickers*

Jump Right In!

1. The Statue of Liberty is 46 meters tall. Her pedestal is 47 meters tall. How tall are the statue and pedestal together?

$$\begin{array}{r} 46 \\ + 47 \\ \hline \end{array}$$

    A. 83 meters

    B. 93 meters

    C. 813 meters

    D. 913 meters

2. The Statue of Liberty's right arm is 42 feet long. Her tablet is about 24 feet long. How many feet long are her arm and the tablet together?

$$\begin{array}{r} 42 \\ + 24 \\ \hline \end{array}$$

    A. 18 feet

    B. 46 feet

    C. 66 feet

    D. 76 feet

3. The Statue of Liberty is made up of 125 tons of steel and 31 tons of copper. How much does the statue weigh?

A. 156 tons

B. 166 tons

C. 420 tons

D. 445 tons

Show your work. Write your answer in a sentence.

4. A guided tour of the Statue of Liberty takes 45 minutes. The ferry ride to the statue takes 15 minutes. How many minutes are the ride and tour altogether?

5. If your class waited in line for 115 minutes, how many total minutes would your class spend in line, on the ferry, and on the tour?

Excellent Job!

 **Checking In**

Answers for pages 150 and 151:

   1. B

   2. C

   3. A

   4. An A+ answer: 45 + 15 = 60. The tour and ferry ride take 60 minutes.

   5. An A+ answer: 115 + 60 = 175. The wait, tour, and ferry would take 175 minutes.

Did your child get the correct answers? If so, review each question and ask, "What numbers did you add first? Why? Which numbers did you add next?"

Did your child get any of the answers wrong? If so, go over the incorrect answers. For question 3, look over your child's work to see if he or she lined up the digits correctly. Ask, "How did you decide how to line up 125 and 31?" Ask your child to tell you the place value of all the digits in both numbers. Then, tell him or her to line up the numbers so each ones digit is in the same column and each tens digits is in the same column. If your child is having trouble with basic addition facts, show your child how to count on his or her fingers.

 **Watch Out!**

In question 1, kids might add 46 and 47 by adding the ones column (6 + 7 = 13) and then adding the tens column (4 + 4 = 8) for an answer of 813. Tell your child to start by adding the digits in the lowest place value (6 ones + 7 ones = 13 ones can be regrouped as 1 ten and 3 ones). Now, your kid can add all the tens, including the regrouped ten.

 **Study Right**

If your child was confused by the word problems, encourage him to read them carefully. Ask your child to point out words that tell him which operation to use. For example, *altogether*, *total*, and *in all* are usually used in word problems to indicate that your child should add.

What to Know...

Addition is a fundamental skill that is important in school and in life.

Review this skill with your child this way:

- **Addition** is an operation that combines numbers.

- The **sum** is the number that results from adding numbers.

There are numbers to add all around us! Your child adds to find out how many points her basketball team has scored in the first two quarters of a game.

Make sure your kid understands why this addition problem uses regrouping. Remind your kid that 3 ones + 8 ones = 11 ones, which can be regrouped as 1 ten and 1 one.

 Checking In

Check that your kid understands how the numbers in this problem are lined up. Make sure he or she understands why the 8 is written underneath the 3 and not underneath the 1. Review the lesson on place value if necessary.

On Your Way to an "A" Activities

Type: Speaking/Listening & Game/Competitive
Materials needed: deck of cards, paper, pencil
Number of players: 2 or more

Take out all of the jokers, jacks, queens, and kings from a deck of cards. Draw three cards to make a three-digit number. Then, draw three more cards to make another three-digit number. (Count an ace as one.) Explain aloud what you are doing as you add the numbers together. Write your work on paper. Then, the next player will do the same. The player with the largest sum gets a point. The first player to get 7 points wins the game!

Type: Game/Competitive
Materials needed: index cards, paper, crayons or pens, O-shaped cereal, or pennies
Number of players: 2–4

Play Math Bingo! Using only the numbers 0 to 10, write two numbers with a plus sign on each index card—but do not write the sum! Next, create your own bingo card by making a table with 4 rows across and 4 columns up and down. Fill it in with the numbers 0 to 20.

Play Math Bingo by choosing one flash card at a time. If you have the sum on your bingo card, place a piece of cereal or a penny on that space. The first player to have 4 in a row wins.

Type: Arts and Crafts
Materials needed: poster board, markers or crayons, materials
Number of players: 1 or more

Create an addition table like the one below.

+	0	1	2	3
0	0	1	2	3
1	1	2	3	4
2	2	3	4	5
3	3	4	5	6

In each box, write the sum of the number in the first column and the number in the first row. For example, the red 4 is the sum of 1 (the row) and 3 (the column). Make your table for the numbers 0 to 10. Use different colors or materials for different numbers—let them show some personality! Decorate your table.

Type: Active
Materials needed: dice, paper, pencil
Number of players: 1 or more

Roll the dice. Add the numbers you rolled, then act out the sum by clapping or stomping out the answer. For example, if you rolled a 3 and a 5, clap your hands 8 times. Write down each sum and choose a different movement each time. Can you think of a different movement for each sum from 2 to 12?

Has your kid breezed through the activities? If so, he or she can work on this Using Your Head activity independently.

Using Your Head

[20] minutes

Grab a **pencil**!

Find the sum for each problem. Write one number from each sum under each line, as shown. Then, use the key below to break the code!

237 + 168 = __405__

39 + 40 = _____

4 + 16 = _____

0 + 6 = _____

27 + 156 = _____

Second Graders Are...

Most second graders enjoy repetition. If your child particularly enjoys one activity, encourage him to play it again!

___ ___ ___ ___ ___ ___ ___
 4   0   5

___ ___ ___

0	1	2	3	4	5	6	7	8	9
	A	E	H	I	L	M	O	T	V

Subtraction

By now, your kid is probably a pro at solving simple problems like 3 – 1. Subtraction with regrouping may be another story. Remembering how—and which numbers—to regroup can be tricky, especially at first. Kids might even be tempted to eliminate the need for regrouping by switching the order of numbers. When faced with 26 – 9, your kid might solve 29 – 6 instead. In school, your kid first learned how to subtract by subtracting a smaller number from a larger number. Because this was how your kid was introduced to subtraction, he or she may think that this is the way it should always be.

Once your kid learns to regroup by trading 1 ten for 10 ones, subtraction will be a breeze.

First things first: Get a sense of what your kid already knows. Turn the page and tell your kid to Jump Right In!

Here's what you'll need for this lesson:

- *cereal, pennies, or beans*
- *crayons or markers (including a red one and a blue one)*
- *paper*
- *pencil*
- *poster board*
- *25 blank index cards*
- *scissors*
- *masking tape*

Jump Right In!

1. The average African elephant is 89 centimeters tall at birth. The average adult cheetah is at least 73 centimeters tall. How many centimeters taller is a baby elephant than an adult cheetah?

$$\begin{array}{r} 89 \\ -73 \\ \hline \end{array}$$

    A. 6 centimeters

    B. 12 centimeters

    C. 16 centimeters

    D. 22 centimeters

2. Greyhounds can run up to 45 miles per hour. The fastest human can run up to 28 miles per hour. How many miles per hour faster can a greyhound run than a human?

$$\begin{array}{r} 45 \\ -28 \\ \hline \end{array}$$

    A. 13 miles per hour

    B. 17 miles per hour

    C. 23 miles per hour

    D. 27 miles per hour

3. Grizzly bears can run up to 30 miles per hour. Pigs can run up to 11 miles per hour. How many miles per hour faster can a grizzly bear run than a pig?

$$\begin{array}{r} 30 \\ -\ 11 \\ \hline \end{array}$$

A. 19 miles per hour

B. 21 miles per hour

C. 29 miles per hour

D. 41 miles per hour

4. Most dogs have 42 teeth. Most humans have 32 teeth. How many more teeth do most dogs have than most humans? Write your answer in a sentence.

5. How much taller is this redwood than this building? Write your answer in a sentence.

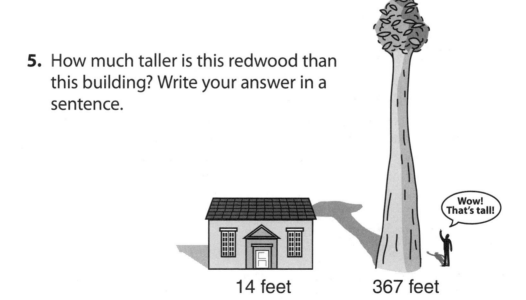

14 feet   367 feet

Excellent Job!

 *Checking In*

Answers for pages 158 and 159:

1. C

2. B

3. A

4. An A+ answer: 42 − 32 = 10. "Dogs have 10 more teeth."

5. An A+ answer: 367 − 14 = 353. "The redwood is 353 feet taller."

Did your child get the correct answers? If so, ask how. Check that he understands subtraction by asking him to explain which digits he subtracted first. Then, ask how he knew when to regroup.

Did your child get any of the answers wrong? Your kid may have tried to subtract the larger digit from the smaller one. Remind your child that she can't change the order of the digits.

 Watch Out!

Regrouping has other challenges too. For example, when solving 45 − 28 in question 2, your kid may have regrouped 4 tens as 4 tens and 10 ones instead of 3 tens and 10 ones. Point out that your child is taking away 1 ten, so the tens digit has to change. Let your kid use cereal or pennies to model these problems. Give her a few subtraction problems with and without regrouping to develop her skills.

 Study Right

Encourage your child to write down the regrouped numbers instead of trying to remember them in his head. For example, in question 2, tell him to cross off the 4 in the tens column and write 3 above it, and then to write a 1 in front of the 5 in the ones column. This way, your child can easily see how many ones and tens there are by looking at the paper.

What to Know...

Subtraction is all around us. Kids need to be comfortable with subtracting both in school and outside it.

Review these skills with your child this way:

- **Subtraction** is a way to take a number away from another number to find the result, or difference.

- The **difference** is the result of subtracting one number from another number.

You and your child can use subtraction to find out how many pieces of candy he or she has left after giving some away.

24 candies
− 9 candies
‾‾‾‾‾‾‾‾‾‾
15 candies

Make sure your kid understands why this subtraction problem needs regrouping. Explain that 2 tens can be regrouped as 1 ten and 10 ones, so 4 ones can be rewritten as 14 ones.

 *Checking In*

Check that your kid understands how the numbers in the problem are lined up. Make sure he or she understands why the 9 is written underneath the 4 and not underneath the 2. Ask your child to name the place value of each digit in the example. Remind him or her that numbers with the same place value should be lined up underneath each other.

On Your Way to an "A" Activities

{ **10** minutes } Type: Reading/Writing
Materials needed: paper, pencil
Number of players: 1 or more

Write a subtraction story. Pick a fun topic—kids at a birthday party, animals in a zoo, cookies being baked, or anything else. In the story, you (or another character) have to subtract 2 things and end up with a difference of 8. Be creative—you can even draw pictures if you'd like.

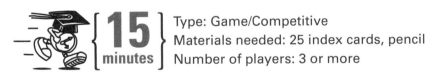

{ **15** minutes } Type: Game/Competitive
Materials needed: 25 index cards, pencil
Number of players: 3 or more

Ask a parent or a friend to write a subtraction problem on each index card. The leader should hold up one card at a time. If the problem requires regrouping, say, "Regroup!" If the problem does not require regrouping, say, "Nope!" The first player to say the correct answer wins the card. The player with the most cards at the end wins the game.

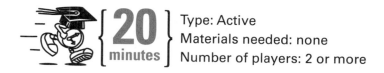

Type: Active
Materials needed: none
Number of players: 2 or more

Pretend you are a hungry animal. You can even make a costume if you like. What kind of animal are you? When you're ready, go looking for food. Gather your food in one place, such as the kitchen table. Pretend some of your food is lost in a rainstorm: how much is left? What if more animals come and want to eat? How will you share your food?

Type: Arts and Crafts
Materials needed: paper, markers or crayons, beans, pennies, or other small items, masking tape, scissors
Number of players: 1 or more

Create your own subtraction poster by writing and solving three different subtraction problems. Use different colors to show any numbers you regroup. Then, show your problems in picture form. For example, you could write "22 – 9 = 13" and glue 22 beans, pennies, or any other small items to your poster. Ask a grown-up to help you cut small pieces of masking tape. Use the strips to make Xs over 9 items to show only 13 remaining. Decorate the poster and hang it up.

Second Graders Are...

Second graders need and enjoy security and structure. Try to have a designated study space, such as the kitchen table or a desk, and a set time every week for using this book. This routine may bring comfort to your child.

Has your child breezed through the activities? If so, he or she can work on this Using Your Head activity independently.

Using Your Head

{ **20** minutes }

*Grab a **red marker** and a **blue marker**!*

Use a blue marker to add. Use a red marker to subtract.

1. A sled dog team has 22 dogs. If 8 dogs leave, how many dogs are left on the team?

2. There are 103 dogs in a park. If 52 more dogs arrive, how many dogs are in the park now?

3. Spike weighs 34 pounds. Muffin weighs 27 pounds. How much do Spike and Muffin weigh together?

4. Fluffy weighs 62 pounds. Max weighs 14 pounds. What is the difference between Fluffy and Max's weights?

Add the blue numbers: _____

Add the red numbers: _____

Use this key to break the code. What is the message? _____

27	62	184	216
cannot	win	have	You

Answers: 1. 14; 2. 155; 3. 61; 4. 48; Blue total: 216; Red total: 62; Code: You win!

164   Cracking the Second Grade

Ways of Representing Numbers

In the past, your kid probably figured out the value of a number by how long it took to count up to that number. If your kid started counting from 1, he or she got to 3 and eventually to 30—and a while later got to 300.

But now, your kid is starting to learn about numbers in a completely different way. Now, your kid knows about place value. So, the digit 3 can occur in the ones place, the tens place, the hundreds place, and so on—and it can be part of a different number each time. It's place-value location that tells the value of the digit.

Our entire number system is rooted in this idea of place value. Your child will use this not only in second-grade math and then in third-grade math, but also in all aspects of life: advanced classes, paying bills, buying groceries, and work.

First things first: Get a sense of what your kid already knows. Turn the page and tell your kid to Jump Right In!

Here's what you'll need for this lesson:
- calculator
- lined paper
- pencil
- tape
- pens

Jump Right In!

1. Toby learned that part of the Grand Canyon is 7,406 feet deep. Which of the following is the same as 7,406?

    A. 7 + 4 + 6

    B. 7,000 + 46

    C. 7,000 + 400 + 60

    D. 7,000 + 400 + 6

2. What number is the same as 3,000 + 400 + 70 + 3?

    A. 347

    B. 472

    C. 3,473

    D. 3,743

3. The Colorado River is 1,450 miles long. Which of the following is the same as 1,450?

    A. 1 + 4 + 50

    B. 100 + 40 + 5

    C. 1,000 + 400 + 50

    D. 1,000 + 40 + 50

Rory and Samantha went on a trip to the Grand Canyon and the Colorado River with their family.

4. Rory read that the canyon is about 277 miles long. What is the same as 277?

5. Samantha counted how many birds she saw at the park. She counted 400 birds, then another 70 birds, and then another 5 birds. She wrote down how many birds she saw. 400 + 70 + 5

What is the same as 400 + 70 + 5?

Excellent Job!

 **Checking In**

Answers for pages 166 and 167:

1. D

2. C

3. C

4. An A+ answer: 200 + 70 + 7

5. An A+ answer: 475

Did your child get the correct answers? If so, ask your child to explain why each of the other answer choices is wrong. For example, answer choice A for question 1 is wrong because 7 + 4 + 6 = 17, not 7,406.

Did your child get any of the answers wrong? If so, he or she might be confused about what to do when there is a 0 in a number. For example, with question 3, explain that the 1 shows that there is 1 thousand (1,000), the 4 shows that there are 4 hundreds (400), the 5 shows that there are 5 tens (50), and the 0 shows that there are no ones (0). Ask your child what the 0 shows in 7,406 (question 1), and make sure your child understands that the 0 shows that there are no tens.

 **Watch Out!**

Understanding the value of zero can be confusing. To help your kid, instruct him or her to write out the value of each digit in a number. For example, with the number 405, your kid could write the following:

"The 4 stands for 4 hundreds. 400.

The 0 stands for 0 tens. 0.

The 5 stands for 5 ones. 5."

Explain to your child that there are no tens, so write a zero in the tens place of the number. If your child becomes confused about the value of a zero, encourage him or her to write out the value of each number this way.

What to Know...

Using place value can help your kid understand the value of numbers.

Review place value skills with your child this way:

- A **digit** is a symbol that is used to write numbers. There are 10 digits: 0, 1, 2, 3, 4, 5, 6, 7, 8, and 9.

- **Place value** is the value of a digit based on its place in a number. For example, in the number 382, the digit 8 is in the tens place, so it has a value of 80.

While visiting a national park, you and your child might come across a tree labeled with the sign shown below.

Thousands	Hundreds	Tens	Ones
1	7	6	7

1,767 years old

1,767= 1,000 + 700 + 60 + 7

Ask your child to name the place value of each digit in the number 1,767. Ask your child to identify the value of each digit. For example, your child might say, "The 1 is in the thousands place. That means the 1 shows 1 thousand."

Your child also uses place value to understand the value of numbers when playing games with money.

thousands	hundreds	tens	ones
5	0	4	7

5000 + 40 + 7 = 5,047

Ask your child to count the number of thousand-dollar bills, hundred-dollar bills, ten-dollar bills, and one-dollar bills. Then, ask your child to identify what digits go into what place values in the place-value chart. For example, your child might say, "There are 5 thousand-dollar bills. That means 5 goes into the thousands place of the number" or "There are no hundred-dollar bills. That means 0 goes into the hundreds place of the number."

Second Graders Are...

Like most people, second graders benefit from frequent and specific positive reinforcement. Remember to encourage your child regularly and make sure that your encouragement accurately points out your child's successes and achievements.

On Your Way to an "A" Activities

{ **15** minutes }
Type: Reading/Writing
Materials needed: calculator, lined paper, pencil
Number of players: 2

Punch a two- or three-digit number, such as 99, into the calculator. Give the calculator to your parent or friend. Your parent or friend reads the number and writes it down, then writes the number broken apart by place value: 90 + 9. Check your parent or friend's work by punching 90 + 9 = into the calculator to see if it matches the original number. Switch jobs and play again.

{ **10** minutes }
Type: Active
Materials Needed: tape, pencil
Number of Players: 2 or more

Start by standing with your back against a wall. Then, the other player should say a large number, such as "Two thousand one hundred sixty-three." Take large steps to show the digit in the thousands place. Now, take regular-sized steps to show the digit in the hundreds place, little steps to show the digit in the tens place, and tiny steps to show the digit in the ones place. When you are done, put a piece of tape down on the floor to show where you ended. Write the number on the piece of tape. For example, for 2,163, you would take two large steps, one regular-sized step, 6 little steps, and 3 tiny steps. Then, you would write 2,163 on the piece of tape. Switch turns, and try different numbers.

Using Your Head

[10 minutes]

Grab a **pencil**!

Find the treasure. For each step, answer the question to find your way to the treasure chest. Solve the final problem and win!

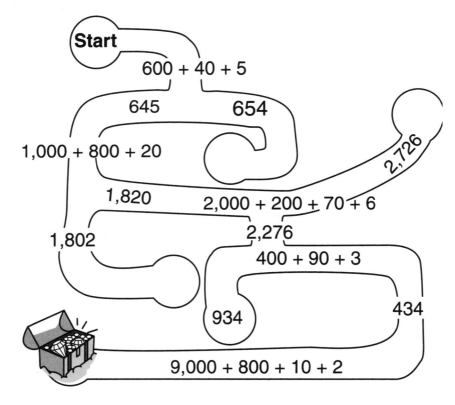

Start

600 + 40 + 5

645   654

1,000 + 800 + 20

2,726

1,820   2,000 + 200 + 70 + 6

1,802   2,276

400 + 90 + 3

934   434

9,000 + 800 + 10 + 2

Answer _____

Multiplication

By now, your kid probably understands that 3 fish + 2 fish means that 3 fish are swimming along and meet 2 more fish for a total of 5 fish. Your kid can probably picture the 3 fish, the 2 other fish, and then the final group of 5 fish.

Multiplication can be tricky for kids because it's the first time that numbers mean groups and not things. For example, 3 × 2 doesn't mean "3 fish times 2 fish"—it means "3 groups of fish with 2 fish in each group." The idea that a number represents groups or sets takes kids time to get used to. If they don't understand the concept of equal groups, kids can misunderstand multiplication.

Once your child does master the concept of equal groups and multiplication, there will be loads of opportunities to use that knowledge—figuring out the total cost of baseball tickets for the family, the number of snacks to get out for friends, and so on. Your kid is sure to love being able to figure these things out quickly and easily. Soon enough, your kid may be begging for chances to help you out using these new whiz-kid skills.

First things first: Get a sense of what your kid already knows. Turn the page and tell your kid to Jump Right In!

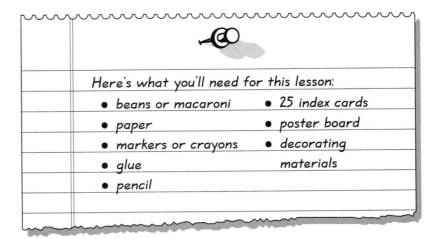

Here's what you'll need for this lesson:
- beans or macaroni
- paper
- markers or crayons
- glue
- pencil
- 25 index cards
- poster board
- decorating materials

Jump Right In!

1. A cook puts 4 sprinkles on each cookie. If the cook makes 6 cookies, how many sprinkles will the cook use altogether?

    A. 2

    B. 10

    C. 20

    D. 24

2. In art class, each student gets 8 crayons. If there are 5 students, how many crayons are needed altogether?

    A. 3

    B. 13

    C. 40

    D. 48

3. $$\begin{array}{r} 3 \\ \times\, 7 \\ \hline \end{array}$$

    A. 10

    B. 21

    C. 30

    D. 37

4. $$\begin{array}{r} 9 \\ \times\, 4 \\ \hline \end{array}$$

    A. 36

    B. 40

    C. 49

    D. 94

Jacob and Maria went to the zoo for a class trip. They saw the zookeepers check the animals to make sure they were healthy. The zookeepers checked the animals' feet to make sure there were no cuts. Use this information to answer questions 5 and 6 below.

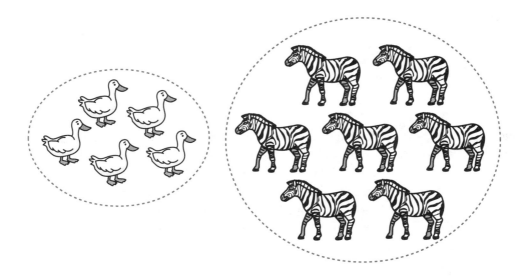

5. Jacob watched the zookeepers check the ducks. Use multiplication to find out how many duck feet the zookeepers checked in all.

   _____ × _____ = _____

6. Maria watched the zookeepers check the zebras. Use multiplication to find out how many zebra feet the zookeepers checked in all.

   _____ × _____ = _____

Excellent Job!

 *Checking In*

Answers for pages 174 and 175:

1. D

2. C

3. B

4. A

5. An A+ answer: 2 × 5 = 10

6. An A+ answer: 4 × 7 = 28

Did your child get the correct answers? If so, find out what method your child used to find the correct answer. Your child may have known the multiplication facts. For example, for question 1, your child may have known that 4 × 6 = 24. However, your child also might have used repeated addition (4 + 4 + 4 + 4 + 4 + 4 = 24) or drawn a picture of 6 cookies with 4 sprinkles each and counted the sprinkles. If your child used one method to answer the questions, explain these other methods. Tell your child that he or she can use many different methods to solve problems or to check his or her answers.

Did your child get any of the answers wrong? If your child got question 1 or 2 wrong but got questions 3 and 4 right, your child may know multiplication facts but have difficulty using them to answer word problems. If your child got question 1 or 2 right and got question 3 or 4 wrong, then your child needs to review basic multiplication facts. Review the questions with your child using the multiplication facts table on page 178. For example, review question 3 by asking your child to put a finger on the 3 in the top row and a finger on the 7 in the left column. Then, instruct your child to move his or her fingers together until they meet (at 21). This is the correct product.

 *Watch Out!*

Kids at this age might be baffled by the idea of using numbers to represent sets. Keep an eye out for your kid adding or subtracting numbers instead of multiplying them.

Using items around the house, make several equal sets (for example, 3 groups of 5 pennies). Ask your child how many groups there are and how many are in each group. Then, ask your child to use multiplication to find the total number of items. Repeat, using different numbers of items.

What to Know...

Your child can use multiplication to figure things out quickly, such as "How many fish are at the pet store?"

Review these skills with your child this way:

- **Equal groups** are groups that all have the same number of objects.

- **Multiplication** is combining equal groups. You can combine equal groups in many different ways.

- The **multiplication sign** is ×. When your child sees ×, he or she should say "times."

- A **factor** is a number multiplied by another number.

- A **product** is a number that is the result of multiplying numbers.

Your child can use basic multiplication facts when working with equal groups.

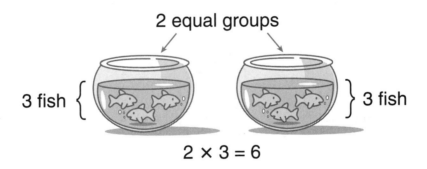

2 equal groups

3 fish   3 fish

$$2 \times 3 = 6$$

 *Checking In*

Make sure your child understands how to write multiplication problems. Ask your child, "What is the number of groups? What is the number in each group?" Remind your child that multiplication is the number of groups times the number in each group.

Your child can use the multiplication facts in the multiplication facts table.

Ask your child to count all the fish in each bowl. Explain that there are 3 fish in each bowl, so these are equal groups of fish. Then, ask your child to identify the factors (2 and 3) and the product (6).

×	0	1	2	3	4	5	6	7	8	9	10
0	0	0	0	0	0	0	0	0	0	0	0
1	0	1	2	3	4	5	6	7	8	9	10
2	0	2	4	6	8	10	12	14	16	18	20
3	0	3	6	9	12	15	18	21	24	27	30
4	0	4	8	12	16	20	24	28	32	36	40
5	0	5	10	15	20	25	30	35	40	45	50
6	0	6	12	18	24	30	36	42	48	54	60
7	0	7	14	21	28	35	42	49	56	63	70
8	0	8	16	24	32	40	48	56	64	72	80
9	0	9	18	27	36	45	54	63	72	81	90
10	0	10	20	30	40	50	60	70	80	90	100

Your child can check his or her answers to multiplication problems by using repeated addition.

3 equal groups

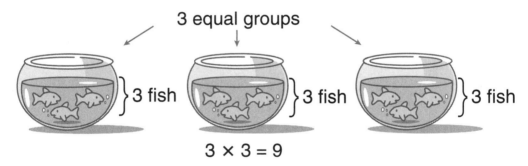

} 3 fish   } 3 fish   } 3 fish

$3 \times 3 = 9$

Ask your child, "How many fish would there be if the pet store had 3 bowls of 3 fish?" Help your child use the multiplication facts table ($3 \times 3 = 9$) and to check the answer using repeated addition ($3 + 3 + 3 = 9$).

Cracking the Second Grade

On Your Way to an "A" Activities

10 minutes

Type: Arts and Crafts
Materials needed: paper, pencils, things around the house
Number of players: 1 or more

Imagine you are writing a grocery list. You need to know how much food and other things to buy. Go around your house and find things that are in equal groups. For example, you can find cartons of eggs that are in equal groups of 12 eggs or packs of toilet paper that are in equal groups of 6 rolls of toilet paper. Write a list of these things. Then, decide how many packs of each thing you would buy. Write a multiplication problem for each. For example, if you wanted to buy 3 cartons of eggs, you would write $3 \times 12 = 36$.

20 minutes

Type: Arts and Crafts
Materials needed: 25 index cards, markers or crayons, glue, beans or macaroni
Number of players: 1 or more

Make your own multiplication flash cards. Use the multiplication facts table on page 178. Write a different multiplication fact on each index card. Then, glue beans or macaroni onto each card to show the multiplication fact. So, for 3×2, you would glue 3 groups of 2 beans. You can look at your flash cards to review multiplication facts.

Using Your Head

*Grab a **pencil** and some **crayons** or **markers**!*

For each multiplication problem, draw a picture of the animal or animals mentioned. Then, find the product.

1. Jacob saw a sloth. The sloth had 4 feet. Each foot had 3 claws. How many claws did the sloth have altogether?

2. Maria saw a cage with 4 birds. Jacob saw another cage with 4 birds. How many birds did they see in all?

3. Maria saw 3 monkeys. Each monkey had 2 bananas. How many bananas were there in all?

Answers: 1. a picture of 1 sloth with 4 feet, each foot with 3 claws, $4 \times 3 = 12$; 2. a picture of 2 cages with 4 birds in each cage, $2 \times 4 = 8$; 3. a picture of 3 monkeys, each with 2 bananas, $3 \times 2 = 6$

Division

Your kid probably has a lot of experience sharing—toys, snacks, TV time, etc. Whenever you've told your kids "Be fair and share equally," you've been getting them to divide.

Your kid has just begun learning about multiplication and division. So, while your kid might know what to do when dividing up snacks, it's easy for him or her to look at a math problem and get these confused. Also, your kid probably knows that multiplication problems involve equal groups, so he or she might assume that any problem involving equal groups means multiplication. Your kid might not realize that he or she can put equal groups together (to multiply) or break up something into equal groups (to divide).

In the future, your child will learn about how multiplication and division are related. For now, your kid needs to be supported when learning how to identify equal groups and how to decide when to multiply or divide. Reminding your child that sharing is a form of division can help your child develop his or her understanding of division.

First things first: Get a sense of what your kid already knows. Turn the page and tell your kid to Jump Right In!

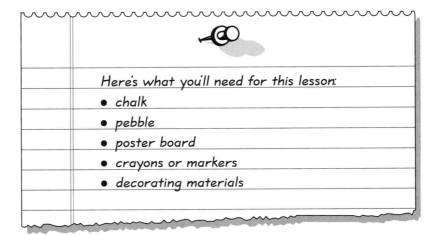

Here's what you'll need for this lesson:
- *chalk*
- *pebble*
- *poster board*
- *crayons or markers*
- *decorating materials*

Jump Right In!

1. A dogsled racer has 2 sleds and 16 dogs. She wants to have the same number of dogs for each sled. How many dogs will be with each sled?

   A. 8

   B. 14

   C. 18

   D. 32

2. A dog trainer has 15 dog treats and 5 dogs. The dog trainer shares the dog treats equally among the dogs. How many treats does each dog get?

   A. 1

   B. 3

   C. 10

   D. 30

3. $10 \div 2 =$

   A. 1

   B. 2

   C. 5

   D. 12

4. $20 \div 4 =$

    A. 4

    B. 5

    C. 16

    D. 24

Lindy and Dray read books about dogs and dogsledding. Use this information to answer questions 5 and 6 below.

5. Lindy read a book about 8 dogs. Draw 8 dogs. Circle equal groups of 4 dogs. Use division to show how many equal groups of dogs there are.

    $8 \div 4 =$ _____

6. Dray read a book about 24 dogs. Draw 24 dogs. Circle equal groups of 8 dogs. Use division to show how many equal groups of dogs there are.

    $24 \div 8 =$ _____

Excellent Job!

A Answers for pages 182 and 183:

1. A

2. B

3. C

4. B

5. An A+ answer: Your child should circle 2 groups of 4 dogs. 8 ÷ 4 = 2.

6. An A+ answer: Your child should circle 3 groups of 8 dogs. 24 ÷ 8 = 3.

Did your child get the correct answers? If so, ask your child how many different ways he or she could find the correct answer. For example, with question 1, your child might know how to use division facts (16 ÷ 2 = 8). Or your child might use repeated subtraction (16 − 2 − 2 − 2 − 2 − 2 − 2 − 2 − 2 = 0; subtracting 2 eight times means 16 divided by 2 is 8). Or your child might have drawn a picture and circled equal groups and then counted the number of equal groups. Make sure your child understands that there are many ways to solve a problem or to check his or her answers.

Did your child get any of the answers wrong? Did your child answer questions 3 and 4 correctly but make a mistake with questions 1 and 2? If so, your child might be familiar with division facts but might be confused by word problems. Review question 2 and ask your child to act out the word problem. Explain that he or she needs to break down a number into equal groups to solve the problem, so he or she can use division. If your child answered question 3 or 4 incorrectly, then he or she may need more review of basic division facts.

Watch Out!

Just like in multiplication, the idea that numbers can represent both groups of things and the things themselves can confuse kids. For example, with question 6, the 3 in 24 ÷ 8 = 3 represents 3 equal groups of dogs (not 3 dogs). If your kid gets this confused, he or she might try to add or subtract to solve this problem, instead of dividing. If this is the case, give your child pennies, beans, or dried macaroni to use when solving division problems. For question 6, your child can count out 24 beans and then count these beans into groups of 8 beans. Your child can then see that there are 3 equal groups of beans.

What to Know...

Every time kids share with others, they're dividing. So, your kid has probably divided a lot without realizing it.

Review these skills with your child this way:

- **Equal groups** are groups that all have the same number of objects.

- **Division** is an operation on two numbers that tells how many groups are in a number. Division also tells how many are in each group.

- The **quotient** is a number resulting from dividing a number by another number. In 24 ÷ 3 = 8, the quotient is 8.

Your kid could use division to share 12 cookies equally among 3 friends.

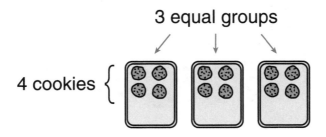

12 cookies ÷ 3 equal groups = 4 cookies

· · · · · · · · · · · · ·

Ask your child to count the cookies on each cookie sheet. Explain that there are 4 cookies on each cookie sheet, so these are equal groups. Then, ask your child to identify the quotient (4).

Your child can memorize basic division facts.

×/÷	0	1	2	3	4	5	6	7	8	9	10
0	0	0	0	0	0	0	0	0	0	0	0
1	0	1	2	3	4	5	6	7	8	9	10
2	0	2	4	6	8	10	12	14	16	18	20
3	0	3	6	9	12	15	18	21	24	27	30
4	0	4	8	12	16	20	24	28	32	36	40
5	0	5	10	15	20	25	30	35	40	45	50
6	0	6	12	18	24	30	36	42	48	54	60
7	0	7	14	21	28	35	42	49	56	63	70
8	0	8	16	24	32	40	48	56	64	72	80
9	0	9	18	27	36	45	54	63	72	81	90
10	0	10	20	30	40	50	60	70	80	90	100

Your child can solve division problems using division facts or using repeated addition.

3 equal groups

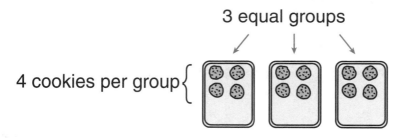

4 cookies per group {

12 cookies ÷ 3 equal groups = 4 cookies
12 cookies − 4 cookies − 4 cookies − 4 cookies = 0 cookies

 Checking In

Kids may have trouble understanding how to use repeated subtraction to solve division problems or how to check their answers to division problems. With the cookie example, your child should keep subtracting 4 cookies from 12 cookies until she gets zero. Then, your child should count the number of times she subtracted 4 cookies. This is the number of groups of 4 cookies, and it is the answer. To help your child, make sure she writes down all the work when using repeated subtraction. That way, your child will be able to know how many times she subtracted.

On Your Way to an "A" Activities

 **15** minutes

Type: Active
Materials needed: chalk and a pebble
Number of people: 2 or more

Draw a long hopscotch playing area on a safe sidewalk. Use different shapes, and make sure the shapes connect. Write a different division problem in each shape (but not the answer). Then, throw a pebble into a shape. Say the answer to the division problem, then hop on one foot to that shape. Take turns. If you don't know the answer, you have to skip your turn. Whoever gets the farthest wins!

 **15** minutes

Type: Arts and Crafts
Materials needed: poster board, markers or crayons, other decorating materials
Number of players: 1 or more

Make an animal division picture story. For example, you could draw 6 dogs and 3 empty doghouses. Then, you could write "$6 \div 3 = 2$" and draw 2 dogs in each house. Decorate your poster. Hang it in your house.

Second Graders Are...

Second graders like to show off what they've learned. Give your kid chances to display and practice his or her talents. If your kid likes the first activity, explain this game to your kid's friends or to neighbors so they can all play together. If your kid enjoys the second activity, encourage your kid to draw a division story in a card for a teacher or grandparent (such as the number of cupcakes shared, or the number of birthday wishes a grandparent can get on each star, and so on).

Has your kid breezed through the activities? If so, he or she can work on this Using Your Head activity independently.

Using Your Head

{20 minutes}

*Grab a **pencil**!*

Solve the problems below by using multiplication or division. Then, use the answers to connect the dots in the picture.

1. Maria has 4 boxes. Each box has 8 markers. How many markers are there altogether?

2. A farmer has 10 pigs and 5 pens. He put the same number of pigs in each pen. How many pigs are in a pen?

3. Jane has 18 marbles and 3 bags. She put the same number of marbles in each bag. How many marbles are in a bag?

4. Sammy has 3 notebooks. Each notebook has 7 stickers. How many stickers are there altogether?

Connect the dots in the order of your answers.

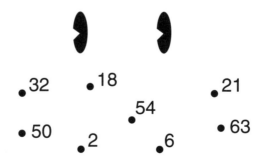

Answers: 1. 32; 2. 2; 3. 6; 4. 21; The dots make a smiley face.

Cracking the Second Grade

Describing Parts

Your kid has probably heard you say, "Bedtime is in half an hour" or "Share half of your dessert with your brother." Fractions are used all the time in everyday life, so your child is probably familiar with them already.

But some of the terms used with fractions—like *numerator* and *denominator*—can sound alien and strange. Most second graders have never heard these words before. Yet these terms can help your kid really understand the details of fractions. While your kid knows what half of his dessert means, that doesn't mean he understands that fractions involve parts of a whole or parts of a group. Your child might be able to apply what he knows about "half" to be able to divvy up "half" of a stack of books or "half" of a pile of pennies. By combining an understanding of the terms *numerator* and *denominator* with real-life experiences, your kid will be on the way to understanding how fractions represent things and to using fractions correctly.

First things first: Get a sense of what your kid already knows. Turn the page and tell your kid to Jump Right In!

Here's what you'll need for this lesson:
- *paper*
- *pencil*
- *Skittles, M&Ms, or any small object that comes in 3 or more colors*
- *10 pennies and 10 dimes*
- *crayons or markers*

Jump Right In!

1. A student drew groups of animals. Which picture shows a group in which $\frac{2}{3}$ of the animals are birds?

   A.

   B.

   C.

   D.

2. Melody had 10 pictures. She looked at 6 pictures. How many of the pictures did she look at?

   A. 4 out of 6

   B. 4 out of 10

   C. 6 out of 10

   D. 6 out of 16

3. Derek had 5 carrots. He ate 1 of the carrots. What fraction of his carrots did he eat?

   A. $\frac{1}{6}$ **C.** $\frac{1}{4}$

   B. $\frac{1}{5}$ **D.** $\frac{4}{5}$

In science class, Tonya and Rick looked for different types of bugs outside. Use this information to answer questions 4, 5, and 6.

4. Tonya and Rick drew a picture of the bugs they saw.

How many ladybugs did they see? _____

How many butterflies did they see? _____

How many bugs did they see in all? _____

5. What fraction of the bugs they saw were ladybugs?

6. What fraction of the bugs they saw were butterflies?

Excellent Job!

 *Checking In*

Ⓐ Answers for pages 190 and 191:

1. A

2. C

3. B

4. An A+ answer: They saw 2 ladybugs, 3 butterflies, and 5 bugs in all.

5. An A+ answer: $\dfrac{2}{5}$

6. An A+ answer: $\dfrac{3}{5}$

Did your child get the correct answers? If so, ask your child to identify the numerators and denominators in all the fractions. For example, in question 3, answer choice A, the 1 is the numerator and the 6 is the denominator. This can help your child become familiar with these terms and learn how to use the terms correctly.

Did your child get any of the answers wrong? If so, review the idea of parts and wholes. For example, with question 1, answer choice A, make sure your child understands that there are a total of 3 animals in the group and 2 of them are birds. The part of the group being asked about is the birds. So, that means that the "part" is the 2 birds and the "whole" is the 3 animals. Have your child write $\dfrac{\text{part}}{\text{whole}}$ as a reminder. Ask your child to use this reminder to identify the correct answer for question 1.

What to Know...

Kids probably don't realize how often they identify parts of a group or parts of a whole in everyday life. Your kid can use fractions for all of these.

Review these skills with your child this way:

- A **fraction** is a number that shows part of a group or part of a whole.
- A **numerator** is the number in a fraction that is above the line. The numerator tells how many parts of the whole are being counted.
- A **denominator** is the number in a fraction that is below the line. The denominator tells how many equal parts are in the whole.

Your kid has probably thought about the parts of a whole cake on birthdays.

Point out that 1 whole cake has been cut into parts. Ask your kid to count the number of slices that are pink and then the total number of slices. Then, ask your kid to identify the numerator and denominator in the fraction.

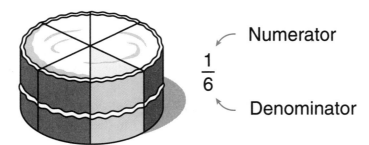

Numerator

$\frac{1}{6}$

Denominator

 *Study Right*

Encourage your kid to make up his or her own mnemonics, or memory devices, for new terms. For example, kids can remember that the *numerator* is above the line and the *denominator* is below the line by remembering that the *d* in *denominator* is for *downstairs*. See if your kid can come up with other ways to remember the terms for this and other concepts.

Your kid has probably thought about the parts of a group when playing games.

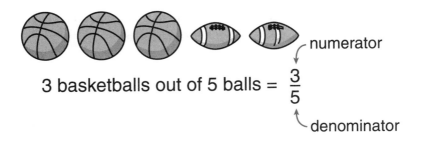

$$3 \text{ basketballs out of 5 balls} = \frac{3}{5}$$

numerator

denominator

Ask your kid to count the number of basketballs and then the total number of balls. Then, ask your kid to identify the numerator and denominator.

Second Graders Are...

Sometimes second graders get excited and rush through their work. Along the way, they might make some mistakes. All that energy needs to be harnessed into an activity so that they can stay focused. Encourage them to put together objects from around the house to match the pictures in the lesson. For example, your child can gather 2 balls for one sport and 3 balls for another to mimic the group of balls in the picture above.

On Your Way to an "A" Activities

Type: Speaking/Listening
Materials needed: none
Number of players: 2 or more

Play "Fraction Surprise!" All the players should stand or sit in a row. One player should step away and come up with a story to say to the other players. This story should also include a question about a fraction. For example, this player could say, "I got new stickers. I got 2 that sparkle and 3 that don't sparkle. What fraction of my stickers sparkle?" Then, this player should quickly pick another player to identify the fraction. If the chosen player correctly says the fraction, this player gets to be the next person who comes up with a story. If this player doesn't name the fraction correctly, another player should be picked until a player gets it right.

Type: Active
Materials needed: objects around the house
Number of players: 2 or more

Play "Fraction Charades." Without speaking, act out or show a fraction. For example, you could gather 5 stuffed animals (3 bears and 2 monkeys) and point to the monkeys. If the other player says $\frac{2}{5}$, he or she gets a point. Take turns until a player gets to 10 points.

Has your kid breezed through the activities? If so, he or she can work on this Using Your Head activity independently.

Using Your Head

{ **10** minutes }

*Grab some **markers** or **crayons**!*

Color in the picture using the following directions:

- Color $\frac{3}{8}$ of the balloons red.

- Color $\frac{1}{4}$ of the gifts yellow.

- Color $\frac{2}{5}$ of the kids' pants blue.

- Color $\frac{3}{5}$ of the kids' pants green.

HAPPY BIRTHDAY!

Answers: 3 red balloons; 1 yellow gift; 2 blue pants; 3 green pants

Shapes

Kids get excited about learning. Once they learn about shapes, they may not be able to stop pointing out shapes everywhere they go. But sometimes at this age, kids don't quite know how to apply their knowledge. For example, your child might learn that triangles have three sides. However, if your child saw a picture of a triangle with sides the same length, then your child might think that ALL triangles must have sides the same length, even though this isn't true. Sometimes it's hard for kids this age to know what details are important and what details aren't as important.

To correctly identify shapes, kids need to know the characteristics of a shape. They also need to hone their organization skills so that they can view and organize details. Guide your child to understand what details to pay attention to. As kids practice, they'll be developing their understanding of shapes and their ability to organize details.

First things first: Get a sense of what your kid already knows. Turn the page and tell your kid to Jump Right In!

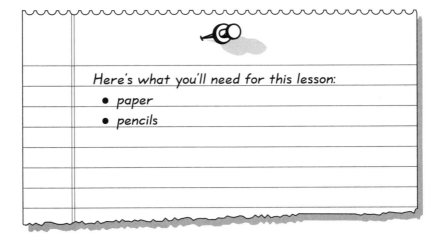

Here's what you'll need for this lesson:
- paper
- pencils

Jump Right In!

1. Which picture is a square?

A.

B.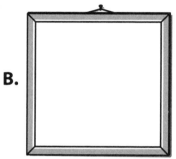

C.

D.

2. What is the name of this shape?

A. rectangle

B. pentagon

C. hexagon

D. octagon

3. Break apart this shape at the dotted line. What two shapes do you get?

A. two squares

B. two triangles

C. two rectangles

D. two pentagons

Martin and Susanna were working together to build a model. The model came with different pieces of wood and directions. Use this information to answer questions 4 and 5.

4. Martin needs to find a piece of wood that has 3 sides. Draw a shape that has 3 sides.

What is this shape?

5. Susanna needs to find a piece of wood that has 6 sides. Draw a shape that has 6 sides.

What is this shape?

Excellent Job!

Checking In

🄐 Answers for pages 198 and 199:

1. B

2. D

3. B

4. An A+ answer: Your child should draw a triangle and write "triangle."

5. An A+ answer: Your child should draw a hexagon and write "hexagon."

Did your child get the correct answers? If so, ask how. Make sure your kid didn't just make some lucky guesses. Check your kid's understanding by asking her to say how many sides and corners each shape has—without looking at her drawing.

Did your child get any of the answers wrong? If so, go over the incorrect answers. Ask your child to draw circles, triangles, squares, rectangles, pentagons, hexagons, and octagons. Discuss how many sides and corners each shape has, and tell your child to label each shape with this information. Let your child refer to these shape drawings while doing questions and activities.

Watch Out!

Kids at this age often have rigid definitions of shapes in their minds. For example, kids often think that all triangles have sides that are the same length. In question 3, the dotted line makes two right triangles—was this confusing to your kid? Help your child by drawing several triangles: a triangle with sides the same length, a right triangle (as in question 3), and other triangles. Explain that any figure with three sides is a triangle.

What to Know...

Shapes are everywhere! Your kid will need practice when learning to identify them correctly, but that practice is easy to come by.

○	A circle is a round shape with no straight sides.
△	A triangle is a shape with three straight sides.
▢	A square is a shape with four square corners and four straight sides. All the sides are the same length.
▯	A rectangle is a shape with four square corners and four straight sides. The opposite sides of a rectangle are the same length.
⬠	A pentagon is a shape with five straight sides.
⬡	A hexagon is a shape with six straight sides.
⯃	An octagon is a shape with eight straight sides.

You and your child can find shapes everywhere.

Your child has probably combined different shapes to make other shapes.

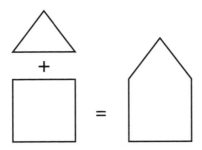

triangle + square = pentagon

Shapes can also break apart into smaller shapes.

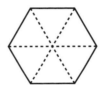

Encourage your child to break apart and put together shapes. Cut out many different shapes from paper for your child. Then, ask your child to cut these shapes into other shapes. For example, your child can cut a square in half diagonally to form two triangles or in half to form two rectangles.

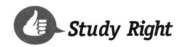 **Study Right**

Emphasize the skill of comparing and contrasting. When answering questions or **doing activities, ask questions, such as, "What do the rectangle and the square have in common? How are they different? How is a square different from a rectangle?" Compare and contrast several different pairs of shapes.**

On Your Way to an "A" Activities

{15 minutes}
Type: Game/Competitive
Materials needed: paper, pencils
Number of players: 2–4

Go on a shape scavenger hunt! On a piece of paper, make a list of shapes. Then, find as many objects as you can that match each shape. Write the name of each object under the shape it matches. A head start: under "rectangle," you can probably list the piece of paper you're writing on! Set a time limit, and whoever finds the most shapes in that time wins.

{15 minutes}
Type: Active
Materials needed: none
Number of players: 4 or more

Become a shape! For example, for a square, you and three friends could lie on the floor, each forming a side. Make sure you're perfectly straight and your corners are right! Have your parent or friend guess what shape you are. How many shapes can you form by yourself? How many can you form with a friend?

Second Graders Are...

At this age, second graders have an increasing interest in the natural world and in classification. Encourage your child by prompting him to name shapes from the natural world with questions such as, "What shape is this honeycomb?" or "What shape is this flower closest to?"

Has your kid breezed through the activities? If so, he or she can work on this Using Your Head activity independently.

Using Your Head

{ **10** minutes }

*Grab some **crayons** or **markers** and a **pencil**!*

Choose a different color for each kind of shape. Color them all in, then write the total number of each shape.

Triangle _____   Hexagon _____

Square _____   Octagon _____

Rectangle _____   Circle _____

Pentagon _____

Which shape isn't in the picture? _____

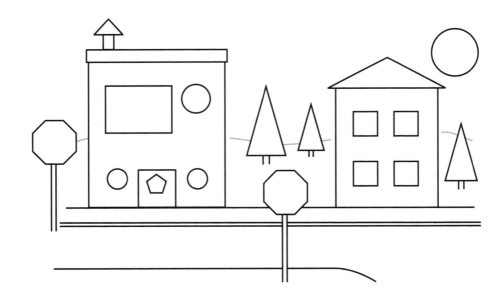

Answers: There are five triangles, five squares, five rectangles, one pentagon, two octagons, and four circles. There are no hexagons in the picture.

Solid Shapes

When your child was a baby, did she call everything that was roundish (a pumpkin, a balloon, even the Moon) a circle or a "ball"? Well, your second grader probably knows that she cannot bounce the Moon, but kids at this age can still have trouble describing three-dimensional shapes.

Although babies begin developing depth perception as early as 2 months of age, they may not develop the vocabulary to distinguish between two-dimensional and three-dimensional shapes until much later. Second graders still tend to describe 3-D objects in terms of flat shapes; for example, they're more likely to say that the Moon is shaped like a circle than like a sphere.

The ability to understand and identify three-dimensional shapes is an important skill. Knowing that 2-D shapes make up the sides, or *faces*, of 3-D shapes will be essential when your child starts learning geometry concepts. For example, your child will need to know that the faces of a triangular pyramid are triangles in order to determine the surface area and understand the basis for volume formulas. These spatial-reasoning skills will also come in handy in everyday life, say, when your kid is trying to figure out the best way to jam all her toys into the toy chest!

First things first: Get a sense of what your kid already knows. Turn the page and tell your kid to Jump Right In!

Here's what you'll need for this lesson:
- *pencil*
- *paper*
- *ruler*
- *scissors*
- *tape*
- *bandanna or necktie*

1. Which figure is a rectangular prism?

A.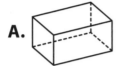

B.

C.

D.

2. What is the name of this shape?

A. pyramid

B. rectangle

C. square

D. cube

3. Which is true for this shape?

A. It has 4 faces.

B. It has 2 faces that are triangles and 3 faces that are rectangles.

C. It has 2 faces that are triangles and 2 faces that are rectangles.

D. All the faces are the same size.

4. Draw a rectangular prism. Then, write how many faces it has. What shapes are they?

5. Think of two objects that are spheres. Then, draw them.

Excellent Job!

 **Checking In**

Answers for pages 206 and 207:

1. A

2. D

3. B

4. An A+ answer: This shape has 6 faces. Each face is a rectangle.

5. An A+ answer: A baseball and an orange could be drawn.

Did your child get the correct answers? If so, ask how. Make sure your kid wasn't just guessing. Ask your kid to name and describe each shape. For questions 3 and 4, ask your kid to explain the word *face*.

Did your child get any of the answers wrong? If so, ask your kid how he or she thought through the question. Ask questions such as, "How did you try to figure out what shape this is? Did you look at the number of faces? Did you look at the shapes of the faces?"

 **Watch Out!**

For question 2, kids may pick answer choice C, square, because each face of a cube has a square shape. Ask your child to draw a square. Place your child's drawing alongside the figure in question 2. Ask your child to explain how the two pictures are alike and how they are different. Guide your kid to see that a square is flat but a cube is not, and that each face of a cube is shaped like a square. If your child is a tactile learner, find some cube-shaped items around your house, such as blocks. Have your child turn over the block (a cube) in his hand, touching all six square faces.

What to Know...

You and your child live in a three-dimensional world and use three-dimensional shapes, such as boxes, balls, and blocks, all the time.

Review geometric solids with your child this way:

Cube	Face	Sphere
six square faces that are all the same size	a flat side of a solid shape	a solid shape with no straight sides like a round ball

Triangular pyramid	Rectangular pyramid
two bases that are triangles and are parallel; the two bases are the same size and shape	six faces that are rectangles

Your kid should recognize these shapes.

sphere

triangular prism

rectangular prism

 **Study Right**

Encourage your kid to look for information in the names of the shapes. Many kids have trouble seeing the difference between a rectangular prism and a triangular prism. Point out that a *rectangular* prism has *rectangles* on both ends (these are called the *bases*). Then, ask your kid what word is hidden in *triangular prism* (triangle). Point out that a *triangular* prism has *triangles* on both ends. The connection between the names and the shapes may be obvious to you, but some kids may not notice on their own.

On Your Way to an "A" Activities

15 minutes

Type: Game/Competitive
Materials needed: bandanna or necktie, household objects
Number of players: you and a parent

Find a bandanna or a necktie that you can use as a blindfold. Sit at a table next to your parent and put on the blindfold. Your parent will hand you an object, and you have to guess what shape it is without looking. Then, take off the blindfold and check to see if you were right!

10 minutes

Type: Game/Competitive
Materials needed: none
Number of players: you and a parent

Have your parent think of a solid object that can be found in your house. Play "20 Questions" with your parent. Start by asking how many faces the object has. Then, ask how many of the faces are rectangles, and so on. Once you figure out the shape of the object, ask other types of questions. For example, you might want to ask, "What room is it in?" Keep asking until you can guess what the object is or you run out of questions.

Type: Game/Competitive
Materials needed: paper, pencils
Number of players: 2–4

Go on a solid shapes scavenger hunt. Find as many solid shapes as you can around the house and outside. Make a list of each item and its shape. For example, write "lemon = sphere" or "shoe box = rectangular prism." (The shape does not have to be exact.) See who can find the most shapes in 10 minutes.

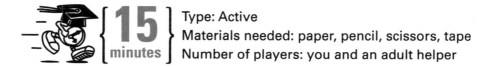

Type: Active
Materials needed: paper, pencil, scissors, tape
Number of players: you and an adult helper

Make your own cube (with help from an adult). Start by tracing the shape below onto a piece of paper. Cut out the shape around the very outside. (Don't cut the dotted lines.) Then, fold the paper at the dotted lines. Tape the sides together to make your own cube.

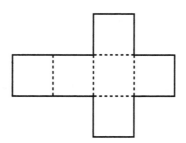

Has your child breezed through the activities? If so, he or she can work on this Using Your Head activity independently.

Using Your Head

[**10** minutes]

*Grab a **pencil**!*

Match each picture with its shape label. You can use each label more than once.

1.

2.

sphere

3.

cube

4.

rectangular prism

5.

triangular prism

6.

7.

Answers: 1. sphere; 2. rectangular prism; 3. rectangular prism; 4. cube; 5. rectangular prism; 6. triangular prism; 7. sphere

Slides, Flips, and Turns

Imagine a crescent shape. Now, imagine flipping this shape over a vertical line and rotating it 90 degrees to the right. What does the shape look like now?

Some people are able to picture this transformation easily, and other people's brains start to hurt just thinking about it. So imagine how second graders must feel. Up until now, geometry has been pretty basic. They've been taught how to identify a bunch of two- and three-dimensional shapes, and the most they've had to do is label them. If it has three sides, it's a triangle; if two of those sides are the same length, it's an isosceles triangle. No problem.

Suddenly, they're expected to look at a triangle, then look at the same triangle after it's been manipulated somehow, and then tell what happened. Now, not only do they have to identify shapes, they also have to compare their orientations and figure out what happened (a slide, a flip, or a turn) to get from figure A to figure B.

This is tough stuff no matter how you slice it. The good news for your child, if he is feeling overwhelmed, is that the spatial reasoning skills he's building in math class will come in very handy outside of school. In fact, you could tell your kid that this is not only math practice, it's also practice for video games!

First things first: Get a sense of what your kid already knows. Turn the page and tell your kid to Jump Right In!

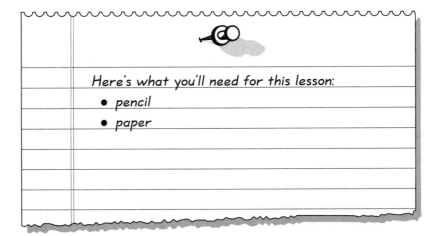

Here's what you'll need for this lesson:
- *pencil*
- *paper*

 **Jump Right In!**

1. What movement does the picture below show?

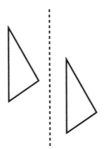

    A. flip

    B. turn

    C. slide

2. What movement does the picture below show?

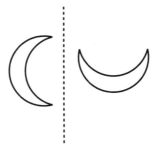

    A. flip

    B. turn

    C. slide

3. Which picture shows a flip?

A.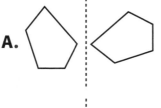

C.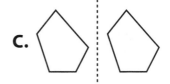

B.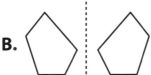

D.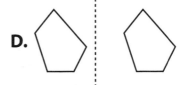

4. Draw this triangle flipped across the line.

5. Use the point to draw this shape turned to the right.

Excellent Job!

 **Checking In**

Answers for pages 214 and 215:

1. C

2. B

3. B

4. An A+ answer: The mirror image of the triangle is drawn.

5. An A+ answer: The shape is rotated to the right.

Did your child get the correct answers? If so, ask how. Make sure your kid wasn't just guessing. Ask, "How is the final shape different from the original shape?" Ask your kid to explain what the terms *flip*, *turn*, and *slide* mean.

Did your child get any of the answers wrong? If so, make sure that he or she understands the term in each question. For example, for question 1, ask, "What does *slide* mean?" Slide this book to the right to illustrate the idea. Then, take the answer choices one at a time. Ask, "What happened to the shape in answer choice A? How did the shape change?" (It was turned to the right.) Then ask, "Is that the same as a slide?" (No.) Turn, slide, and flip the book to show how the terms are different. Then, ask your kid to turn, slide, and flip a different object to check that she understands the terms.

 **Watch Out!**

Kids at this age are still mastering their shapes, so looking at the page and seeing the same shape oriented five different ways can be overwhelming. In question 3, look at each answer choice individually, covering up the other choices with a sheet of paper. Praise your kid if he can name the shape (pentagon), then ask him what happened to the pentagon in answer choice A. If he is having trouble, ask him to pick a particular part of the shape, such as one side of the pentagon, and ask how that side has moved. Help your child see that the whole shape has turned in choice A, then walk through the other answer choices.

What to Know...

The terms *slide, flip,* and *turn* describe movements (in geometry, these are called *transformations*) of shapes.

Review these skills with your child this way:

- A **line** is ←――――――→

- A **point** is ●

Transformation	Definition	Illustration
slide	move along a line	◁ ↕ ◁
flip	move over a line	◁ ↕ ▷
turn	move around a point	◁ ● △

You and your child see slides, flips, and turns all the time.

flip   slide   turn

Ask your kid to explain how each example fits the definition of flip, slide, or turn.

 *Checking In*

Make sure your kid really understands the terms and understands the difference between each term. Ask your kid to explain slides, flips, and turns in her own words. It is important for your child to understand that the shape itself does not change; only the position of the shape changes. To reinforce this point, ask your child to slide, flip, and turn a few objects you find around the house.

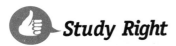 *Study Right*

As you and your child go through these examples, have your child work on his or her attention to detail. Ask your child to describe each picture carefully. Ask questions, such as, "What shape is in the picture? How many points, or corners, does the shape have? In which direction do the points face? How is the other shape different?"

Second Graders Are...

Second graders are developing their own interesting personalities and enjoy telling stories about themselves. Because slides, flips, and turns have almost the same meaning in the real world as they do in math class, ask your child to tell you a story about a time that he or she slid, flipped, or turned something. You can start the conversation by saying something like, "Last night I was having trouble sleeping, so I kept flipping over in my bed. Do you have any of your own stories about flips, slides, or turns?" Having your kid make a personal connection is a good way to reinforce the vocabulary.

On Your Way to an "A" Activities

Type: Game/Competitive
Materials needed: objects around the house (optional)
Number of players: 2 or more and a parent

Play "Simon Says." Your parent will tell you to slide, flip, or turn a body part or an object. If your parent says "Simon says," you should follow the direction. But, if your parent doesn't say "Simon says," you should stay still. You are out if you make the movement without the direction "Simon Says." Play until only one player is left standing.

Type: Reading/Writing
Materials needed: pencil, paper
Number of players: 2 or more

Draw a shape, then draw a slide, flip, or turn of that shape. Have your friend do the same. Then, swap papers and guess what your friend drew: was it a slide, flip, or turn?

Write a sentence explaining your guess. Then, swap papers back. Read your friend's guess and explanation. Was your friend right? Did you guess correctly? If you were right, give yourself a point and play again.

Has your child breezed through the activities? If so, he or she can work on this Using Your Head activity independently.

Using Your Head

{**15** minutes}

*Grab a **pencil**!*

Follow the directions below and draw your answers on the lines given.

И •   Turn halfway around.   _____

H •   Make a $\frac{1}{4}$ turn to the right.   _____

Ɔ ↕   Flip across the line.   _____

Ǝ ↕   Flip across the line.   _____

OW ↕   Flip across the line.   _____

Я ↕   Flip across the line.   _____

ʞ •   Make a $\frac{1}{4}$ turn to the right.   _____

i ↔   Flip across the line.   _____

Answer: The letters spell out "NICE WORK!"

Patterns with Shapes

Second graders are pretty familiar with identifying simple patterns. If they see a wallpaper pattern that goes "dog, cat, dog, cat," they probably know that the rule is "dog, cat." But when it comes to more complicated patterns, second graders' natural enthusiasm can hinder them. Sometimes, they can get so excited that they can stumble, make mistakes, or miss crucial details. For example, if your child sees wallpaper with a pattern that goes "big dog, little dog, cat," there's a good chance she may pay more attention to seeing dogs than to the fact that the dogs are different sizes.

Just as when they cross the street or run in the playground, kids needs to learn to take a second and really look at what's around them. Kids this age are learning to identify when they need to slow down and process all the details they're taking in. When it comes to identifying mathematical patterns, little details are important. Honing your child's ability to process these details can make a big difference!

First things first: Get a sense of what your kid already knows. Turn the page and tell your kid to Jump Right In!

Here's what you'll need for this lesson:
- *pencil*
- *paper*
- *ink pads and rubber stamps*

1. What is the next shape in this pattern?

 A. △   **C.** ◯

 B. ▯   **D.** ▢

2. What are the next two shapes in this pattern?

 A. ⬠◯   **C.** ◯⬠

 B. ⬠▢   **D.** ▢⬠

3. What is the rule for the pattern below?

 A. triangle, triangle

 B. circle, triangle, circle

 C. small triangle, big triangle, circle, circle

 D. big triangle, small triangle, circle

Larry and Mona are getting new scarves for winter. Use this information to answer questions 4, 5, and 6 below.

4. Mona picked out the scarf in the picture. What is the rule for this pattern?

5. Larry saw that there was a shape missing at the end of the pattern. Draw the missing shape.

6. Larry decided he wanted a scarf with the same pattern as Mona's scarf. Draw a picture of Larry's scarf.

Excellent Job!

 *Checking In*

Answers for pages 222 and 223:

1. C

2. B

3. D

4. An A+ answer. The rule is triangle, circle.

5. An A+ answer. Your child should draw a circle.

6. An A+ answer. Your child should draw a scarf with the following pattern: triangle, circle, triangle, circle, etc.

Did your child get the correct answers? If so, ask your child to identify patterns around the house and then identify the rules for those patterns.

Did your child get any of the answers wrong? If so, review the terms *pattern* and *rule* with your child. For example, for question 1, explain to your child that a pattern is a series of shapes that repeats. Point out how the rectangle, circle, and triangle repeat. Explain that the rule for this pattern is "rectangle, circle, triangle" because those are the shapes that always repeat. Ask your child to find the repeating shapes in question 2 and to identify the rule (pentagon, square, pentagon, circle).

 *Study Right*

Writing down lists of observations is a great study skill. When looking for a rule for a pattern, tell your kid to write down a description of each shape in the pattern (such as "big triangle" or "circle"). Your kid might find it easier to read her list of observations and look for descriptions that repeat in order to find a rule. Alternatively, if your kid is a visual learner, ask her to underline or circle each unit of the pattern.

What to Know...

Your kid sees patterns everywhere.

Review these skills with your child this way:

- A **pattern** is a series of numbers, figures, or pictures that follows a rule.
- A **rule** is a statement that tells how the items in a pattern are related.

You or your child might have clothes with patterns like these.

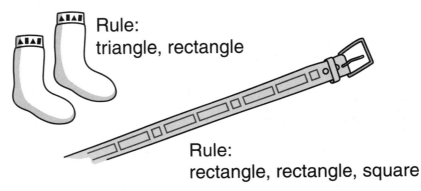

Rule:
triangle, rectangle

Rule:
rectangle, rectangle, square

 *Checking In*

Ask your child to identify what shapes repeat in the socks. Then, tell your child that this is the rule to the pattern. Ask your child to circle the repeating shapes on the belt and identify the rule to the pattern on the belt.

Make sure your child understands how to use a rule to predict the next shape in a pattern. For example, with the sock pattern, explain that the rule "triangle, rectangle" is complete on the sock, so the next shape would be the first shape in the rule. Ask your child to predict the next shape that should appear in the sock pattern (triangle).

Then, discuss the pattern on the belt. If your child hasn't already circled the repeating shapes on the belt, have him do so now. Ask your child to predict the next shape that should appear on the belt (rectangle). If he needs a tip, ask him what comes after the square in the rule for the belt (a rectangle).

Second Graders Are...

Second graders love to discover things. Tell your child that finding a rule is like breaking a code. Encourage your child to "crack the code!" when figuring out the rules to patterns.

On Your Way to an "A" Activities

15 minutes

Type: Game/Competitive
Materials needed: paper, pencil
Number of players: 2 or more

Go on a pattern hunt in your house. Good places to look are on tiles and wallpaper or furniture. Write the rule for the pattern on a piece of paper. Whoever finds the most patterns wins!

20 minutes

Type: Arts and Crafts
Materials needed: paper, ink pads and rubber stamps, stickers, paper grocery bags, scissors, crayons or markers
Number of players: 1 or more

Make your own patterns with rubber stamps or stickers. Or, you can draw a pattern with crayons or markers. First, think about what your pattern will be (for example, "two ducks, one cat"). Then, draw your pattern using stamps, stickers, crayons, or markers. Use your pattern to decorate your notebooks or this book. You can even make your own paper for letter writing by stamping the pattern along the sides of a blank piece of paper. If you have paper grocery bags, cut them open and put your pattern on the blank inside of the bag—you can use this for wrapping paper!

Type: Reading/Writing
Materials needed: paper, pencil, crayons or markers
Number of players: 2 or more

Make word patterns. Write a rule for a pattern with words, such as, "bunny, bear, buffalo: the rule is the words must be kinds of animals that begin with the letter 'b.'" The other players will write their own word patterns. Then, swap papers. Each person should draw the rule he or she has been given. Then, predict the next shape and draw the next shape in the pattern. Look at everyone's drawings. Check to make sure that everyone correctly predicted the next shape. If someone didn't, work together to figure out the next shape in the pattern.

Type: Active
Materials needed: none
Number of players: 2 or more

Play "Wild and Crazy Patterns!" One player can make a sound pattern. For example, this player can make the pattern "clap, clap, stomp, clap, clap, stomp." You can also make action patterns. For example, a player can make the pattern "wink, wink, wave, hop, wink, wink, wave, hop." Once a player has made a wild and crazy sound pattern or action pattern, the other players should make the same pattern. Take turns coming up with the wildest and most difficult patterns.

Has your child breezed through the activities? If so, he or she can work on this Using Your Head activity independently.

Using Your Head

*Grab a **pencil**!*

Find five patterns in the picture below. Write the rule for each pattern.

Pattern: _____

Pattern: _____

Pattern: _____

Pattern: _____

Pattern: _____

Patterns with Numbers

Dealing with the unfamiliar can be scary. By now, second graders are probably used to seeing numbers with addition and subtraction signs. They've gotten used to the idea of seeing two numbers and a sign that tells them what to do. However, a long list of numbers without any kind of sign? They probably haven't seen that before. Having to figure out the hidden relationship between a bunch of numbers can be difficult and confusing for kids.

Kids shouldn't have to think of patterns as scary. Patterns can be fun. Kids at this age love cracking codes. (Just look at the back of your kid's cereal box—there's probably a code game there.) Explain to your kid that finding the rule for a number pattern is like cracking a code. Helping your kid understand that there's a relationship between the numbers will help him or her understand the underlying principles of patterns.

First things first: Get a sense of what your kid already knows. Turn the page and tell your kid to Jump Right In!

Here's what you'll need for this lesson:
- *pencil*
- *paper*
- *crayons or markers*
- *pennies or counters (beans or dried macaroni)*

Jump Right In!

1. What is the rule for the pattern below?

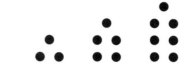

   A. add 1

   B. add 2

   C. add 3

   D. add 4

2. What is the rule for the pattern below?

   4, 7, 10, 13, 16

   A. add 1

   B. add 2

   C. add 3

   D. add 4

3. What is the next number in this pattern?

   5, 10, 15, 20, _____

   A. 21

   B. 23

   C. 25

   D. 30

Cracking the Second Grade

4. What is the next number in this pattern?

2, 9, 16, 23, _____
A. 7
B. 24
C. 25
D. 30

Ron and Rosa went to their friend's birthday party. They were looking for their friend's house. Use this information to answer questions 5 and 6.

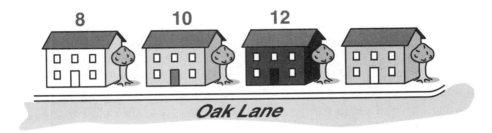

Oak Lane

5. Look at the house numbers. They form a pattern. What is the rule to this pattern?

6. What is the number of the pink house?

Excellent Job!

Checking In

A Answers for pages 230 and 231:

1. B

2. C

3. C

4. D

5. An A+ answer: "The rule for the pattern is 'add 2.'"

6. An A+ answer: "The pink house is number 14."

Did your child get the correct answers? If so, see if your kid can apply these skills to identify a missing number in a pattern. Put your finger over a number in any of the patterns for questions 1–4. Ask your child to identify the missing number.

Did your child get any of the answers wrong? If so, your child may not understand how to identify a rule in a pattern. Demonstrate identifying the rule for question 3. For example, you could say, "I know the first number is 2 and the second number is 9. What would I have to add to 2 to get 9? I know that 2 + 7 = 9. Let's add 7 to the second number. Yes, 9 + 7 = 16. Let's try this rule with the third number. Yes, 16 + 7 = 23. So, 'add 7' is the rule for this pattern." If your child got questions 1 and 2 correct but question 3 or 4 incorrect, then your child might be able to identify a rule but not apply the rule correctly. If so, demonstrate applying the rule. For example, with question 3, you could say, "I know the rule is to add 7. So, I can add 7 to the last number to get the next number. 23 + 7 = 30. So the next number must be 30."

Watch Out!

Did your kid think the rule was always "add 1"? This is a common error. Kids are so used to seeing lists of numbers (0, 1, 2, 3, etc.) that always increase by 1 that they often assume any list of numbers like this increases by 1. The more often your kid sees different patterns, the less likely he or she is to assume every pattern increases by 1. Point out patterns with numbers and identify the rules. For example, you might point out how house numbers are a pattern with the rule "add 2," how the gate numbers at a stadium are in a pattern with the rule "add 10," and so on.

What to Know...

Kids may not be familiar with the term *number pattern*. However, if they've baked batches of cookies or bought packs of pencils, they've used number patterns.

Review these skills with your child this way:

- A **pattern** is a series of numbers, figures, or pictures that follows a rule.

- A **rule** is a statement that tells how the items in a pattern are related.

Let's say your child has several unopened packages of star-shaped stickers, plus one package with only 3 stickers left. She can arrange the stickers as shown below to create the number pattern 3, 11, 19, 27. She can clearly see the rule for the pattern is to add 8.

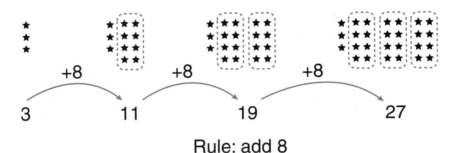

Rule: add 8

 *Study Right*

Tell your kid that he or she can try guessing and checking to find number patterns. For example, your kid can guess that the rule is "add 1." Then, he or she should check this guess by adding 1 to a number in the pattern to see if it results in the next number in the pattern. If it does, keep trying out the rule for all the numbers. If it doesn't, guess again. Tell your child not to become discouraged if his or her first few guesses don't work—he or she can keep guessing and checking.

Ask your kid, "What can be added to 3 to get 11?" Then, ask your kid, "What can be added to 11 to get 19?" Explain that a rule should work for the entire pattern. Then, ask your child to predict how many stickers there will be if an additional package of stickers is added. Tell your child to use the rule to predict the next number in the pattern.

On Your Way to an "A" Activities

{ **20** minutes }

Type: Speaking/Listening
Materials needed: none
Number of players: 2 or more

With the other players, pick a number less than 10. Then, pick a rule, such as "add 2," "add 3," "add 4," or "add 5." The first player should say the number. The next player should use the rule to find the next number. Take turns using the rule to find the next number. See how far you can get!

{ **15** minutes }

Type: Game/Competitive
Materials needed: none
Number of players: 2 or more

Play "Clapping Patterns!" First, pick a number from 1 to 5. Then, pick a rule, such as "add 2," "add 3," or "add 4." Clap out the pattern, stopping in between. For example, if you picked the number 3 and the rule "add 2," you'd clap 3 times, stop, clap 5 times, stop, clap 7 times, stop. Then, see if the other players can guess the rule and clap out the next number in the pattern. Any player that does gets a point. Take turns clapping out patterns and earning points. After every player has had a chance to clap out a pattern, count the points. The player with the most points wins.

Type: Reading/Writing
Materials needed: pencil, paper, crayons or markers
Number of players: 2 or more

Write a pattern of numbers on your paper. Have a friend write a pattern too. Then, switch papers. Draw pictures to show each number. Then, write the rule for your friend's pattern. Have your friend draw pictures and write the rule for your pattern. Then, talk about your patterns to see if you're right.

Type: Active
Materials needed: paper, pencil, pennies or counters (beans or dried macaroni)
Number of players: 2 or more

Play "Bank." Imagine there are 3 banks. For the first bank, write the rule "add 1" on a piece of paper. For the second bank, write "add 2" on a piece of paper. For the third bank, write "add 5" on a piece of paper. Put a penny at each bank. Then, work with the other players to use the rule three times at each bank. Use pennies to figure out the pattern. For example, at the first bank, you'd end up with 1 penny, a pile of 2 pennies, a pile of 3 pennies, and a pile of 4 pennies. Do this for all the banks. Compare how much money you have at the end.

Second Graders Are...

Most second graders need to move around every now and then. Their concentration, both in and out of the classroom, improves when they are allowed to be active for even a few moments. Feel free to break up the lessons by jumping ahead to do an active activity.

Using Your Head

*Grab a **pencil** and some **markers** or **crayons**!*

Ron and Rosa went to a baseball game. Look at the pattern of seats at different baseball stadiums. Identify the rule for each pattern, and draw a line from the pattern to the rule. Then, use the rule to draw the next row of seats.

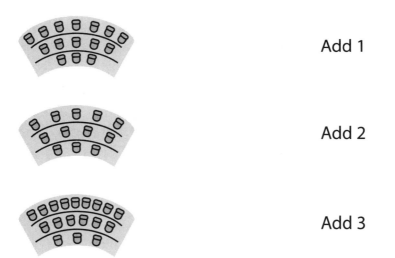

Add 1

Add 2

Add 3

Measuring Length

Second graders often enjoy using tools. Using a ruler to measure things can be thrilling for them. Kids sometimes get so excited about measuring that they treat a ruler like a magical object. They just hold the ruler up to an item and look to the right for the length. Presto—that's the measurement, right?

In their excitement, kids often forget how to use their rulers properly by lining up the left side of an item with the 0 on the ruler. Kids might accurately read the number that lines up with the right side of the item, but it won't be a correct measurement if the left side of the item isn't aligned to 0. Kids often get frustrated and confused when they hear that the length of an item isn't 2 inches when they have clearly seen the right side line up with the big 2 on the ruler.

Measuring length is still a relatively new skill for kids. To measure length correctly, your kid needs practice, especially on how to line up a ruler and how to read the different markings on a ruler.

First things first: Get a sense of what your kid already knows. Turn the page and tell your kid to Jump Right In!

Here's what you'll need for this lesson:
- *rulers with inches and centimeters*
- *tape*
- *paper*
- *pencil*
- *crayons or markers*

Jump Right In!

1. 1 foot =

   A. 10 inches

   B. 12 inches

   C. 36 inches

   D. 100 inches

2. 1 meter =

   A. 1 centimeter

   B. 10 centimeters

   C. 100 centimeters

   D. 1,000 centimeters

3. What is the length of this pencil?

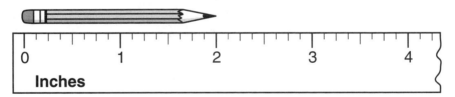

   A. 1 inch

   B. 2 inches

   C. 3 inches

   D. 4 inches

4. What is the length of this worm?

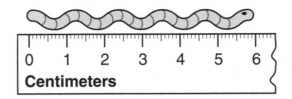

A. 2 centimeters

B. 3 centimeters

C. 4 centimeters

D. 6 centimeters

Enrique and Linda were putting a train set together. They were reading the directions to the train set.

5. Enrique needs to measure the train cars. How long is this train?

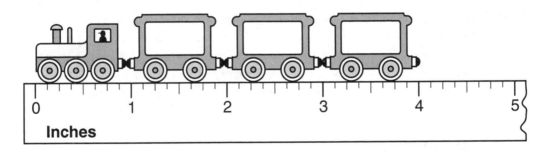

6. Linda is putting together the train tracks. She needs to find a piece of train track that is 9 centimeters long. Use a ruler to draw a train track that is 9 centimeters long.

Excellent Job!

Checking In

1. B

2. C

3. B

4. D

5. An A+ answer: 4 inches

6. An A+ answer: Your child should draw a train track that is 9 centimeters long.

Did your child get the correct answers? If so, ask your child to discuss when he or she has used or could use measurement. If your child knows only that this skill is used in math class, point out examples when this skill is used in the everyday world—with arts and crafts or in careers such as carpentry, clothing design, engineering, etc.

Did your child get any of the answers wrong? If so, discuss all of the questions with your child to help your child identify his or her areas of strength and weakness. For question 1, ask, "Have you ever used inches before?" and "Have you ever talked about how many inches are in a foot before?" For question 2, ask, "Have you ever used centimeters before?" and "Have you ever talked about how many centimeters are in a meter before?" For questions 3 and 5, ask, "Have you ever measured anything in inches before?" For questions 4 and 6, ask, "Have you ever measured anything in centimeters before?"

Watch Out!

Kids at this age sometimes hold the ruler with their entire left hand, covering up the 0. Then, they line up the item with the edge of their hands because that's where they see the numbers start. Demonstrate how to hold a ruler properly using your index finger on the top and your thumb on the bottom. Emphasize lining up the left edge of the object with the 0 on the rule. Ask your kid to practice holding a ruler correctly while measuring small things around the house, like toy cars and sticks of gum.

What to Know...

Your kid is probably more familiar with inches than with centimeters, but he or she needs to be comfortable with both systems of measurement.

Review these skills with your child this way:

- The **American system of measurement** is a system of measurement commonly used in the United States. Inches, feet, and yards are units of length in the American system of measurement.

- The **metric system of measurement** is a system of measurement used around the world. Centimeters and meters are units of length in the metric system of measurement.

Remind your child to do the following when measuring:

- Turn the ruler so the correct units are on top.

- Line up the left side of the item with zero.

- Read the number on the ruler that lines up with the right side of the item.

Ask your kid to use a ruler to measure his or her toys, first in inches and then in centimeters.

You and your child can use the American system or the metric system to measure just about anything.

about 5 centimeters

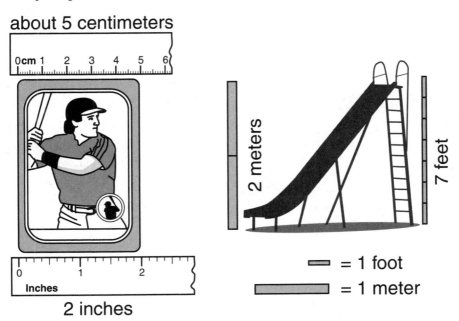

2 inches

= 1 foot

= 1 meter

Kids can get different units confused until they understand the relationship between units.

American Units

12 inches = 1 foot

3 feet = 1 yard

36 inches = 1 yard

Metric Units

100 centimeters = 1 meter

 Study Right

Encourage your child to answer measurement problems with units. Instead of saying the wheel of the train is 2, he or she should say that it is 2 centimeters. Explain to your child that the units are important because there are many units of measurement, so "2" could mean 2 meters, 2 centimeters, 2 feet, 2 inches, etc.

· · · · · · · · · · · · · ●●

To really get a grasp on different units, your child needs to be able to *see* the differences. If you have a yardstick, look at it together with your child. Point out the length of a yard in comparison to the length of a foot and the length of an inch. Then, point out the length of a meter in comparison to the length of a centimeter. Encourage your child to count the units (12 inches in a foot, 100 centimeters in 1 yard, and so on).

On Your Way to an "A" Activities

10 minutes

Type: Active
Materials needed: ruler and tape
Number of players: 2 or more

Measure yourself! Stand against a wall. Your partner should put a piece of tape on the wall at the height of your head. First, find your height in feet and then in inches. Now, measure your partner.

10 minutes

Type: Reading/Writing
Materials needed: pencil and paper
Number of players: 1 or more

Write a poem about measurement. For example:

> The American system uses inches and feet.
> 12 inches per foot. Now, isn't that neat?

Now, see if you can write one about how there are 3 feet in a yard or about how there are 100 centimeters in a meter.

20 minutes

Type: Game/Competitive
Materials needed: rulers
Number of players: 2 or more

Play "Ones." Find objects in your house that are exactly 1 inch, exactly 1 centimeter, and exactly 1 foot long. The first person to find all three wins. The other players should measure the winner's objects to check the measurements.

Using Your Head

[**15** minutes]

*Grab a **pencil**, a **ruler,** and some **crayons** or **markers**!*

Using a ruler, draw each of the pictures described below. Then, use the clues to finish your pictures.

1. Draw a 6-centimeter toy train.

2. Draw a 5-inch toy train.

Clues:

- The longer toy train should be carrying people. Draw people in it.

- The shorter toy train should be carrying food. Draw food in it.

Answers: 1. A 6-centimeter toy train with food in it; 2. A 5-inch toy train with people in it.

244   Cracking the Second Grade

Charts and Graphs

Kids at this age love working with codes. And you know that using charts and graphs is like breaking a code. But it's possible that your child looks at a chart and can't see the code or becomes confused.

For example, your kid might not be familiar with graphs with different increments. He or she may have used only graphs that go from 0 to 1, 1 to 2, and so on. So, when encountering a graph with increments of 2 or 5, your kid might not notice or might become confused. Also, pictographs have keys. If your kid doesn't know to look at the key or how to use the key, he is likely to misunderstand pictographs entirely—this can create a lot of frustration. Your kid may start to believe that he can't do charts and graphs, or your kid may start to feel that charts and graphs don't give him a way into the information.

Luckily, you're here to tell your kid that all the information he needs to understand a chart or graph is already there. That means your kid just needs to learn how to break the code, and that can be a whole lot of fun. Encourage your kid to look for clues to the code—reading the title of the chart and the names of the axis, checking out the increments, and looking at the key.

Charts and graphs are used to display all kinds of important facts and information. For your kid, learning how to understand tally charts, pictographs, and bar graphs can help her know that she can "crack the code" of any charts and graphs she finds in the future.

First things first: Get a sense of what your kid already knows. Turn the page and tell your kid to Jump Right In!

Here's what you'll need for this lesson:

- *paper*
- *pencil*
- *newspapers, magazines, or various household items*

- *crayons or markers*
- *glue*
- *macaroni*
- *other art supplies*

 **Jump Right In!**

Use the tally chart to answer questions 1 and 2.

Team	Points
Wolves	~~HHH~~ ~~HHH~~
Bears	~~HHH~~ ~~HHH~~ ~~HHH~~
Lions	~~HHH~~ ~~HHH~~ ~~HHH~~ ~~HHH~~

1. How many points did the Bears score?

   A. 5

   B. 10

   C. 15

   D. 20

2. Which team had the highest score?

   A. the Bears

   B. the Wolves

   C. the Lions

   D. the Tigers

Use the pictograph to answer question 3.

Favorite Flavors

Chocolate	🍦 🍦 🍦
Vanilla	🍦 🍦 🍦 🍦
Strawberry	🍦

Key	🍦 = 5 students

3. How many students picked vanilla as their favorite?

    A. 4

    B. 5

    C. 20

    D. 25

Mark and Mariah played a game with their dad. They wanted to put the scores from the game into a bar graph. Use this information to answer questions 4 and 5.

4. Mark scored 12 points. Mariah scored 16 points. Their dad scored 14 points. Fill in the bar graph below.

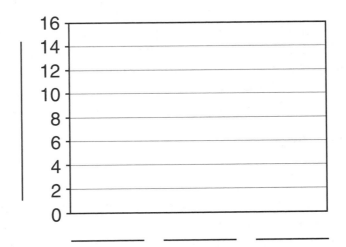

5. Who won the game?

Excellent Job!

 *Checking In*

Answers for pages 246 and 247:

1. C

2. C

3. C

4. An A+ answer: The bar for Mark should show 12 points, the bar for Mariah should show 16 points, and the bar for their dad should show 14 points.

5. An A+ answer: Mariah won the game.

Did your child get the correct answers? If so, ask your child to try to put the information from the tally chart (from questions 1 and 2) into a pictograph or a bar graph.

Did your child get any of the answers wrong? If so, review each chart and graph. For the tally chart, ask your kid, "What does each line in a tally mean?" Or point to the Tigers' score and ask, "What does this group of tally marks mean?" For the pictograph, say, "Look at the key. What is the value of one cone?"

 Watch Out!

For question 3, did your kid think 4 students picked vanilla? If so, your kid probably thought 1 picture means 1 student. Explain that each picture means a certain number of students. Tell your kid to look at the key. Explain that the key says 1 picture of a cone represents 5 students. Then, ask your kid to count how many pictures are in the graph for "vanilla" (4). Because each picture is worth 5, your kid can count by 5 to find the correct answer. Count each picture with your kid to get the correct answer (5, 10, 15, 20). Remind your child that he or she needs to check the key of each pictograph because every pictograph will have a different key.

What to Know...

Tally charts, pictographs, and bar graphs make information and facts easy for your kid to read.

Review these skills with your child this way:

- A **tally** is a way of counting by making a mark for each item counted.
- A **tally chart** is a table that shows data with tally marks.
- A **pictograph** is a graph that shows data by using picture symbols. Each pictograph has a key that tells how many items each symbol represents.
- A **bar graph** is a graph that shows data by using bars of different sizes.

Your child might count the points in a game using a tally chart.

Player	Points
Me	ЖЖ ЖЖ ІІ
My Friend	ЖЖ ІІІ

 **Study Right**

. . . . ●
Ask your kid to count the tally marks to find out how many points each person has.

Encourage your kid to read the titles, labels, and key of each graph before he or she starts to answer questions. Model this behavior for your child as you work through this lesson.

In school, your child's teacher might make a pictograph or a bar graph to show how many days each student did a classroom chore.

▸ Pictograph

Cleaned Class Desks

Aaron	🪑 🪑 🪑 🪑
Beth	🪑 🪑
Angel	🪑 🪑 🪑

Key	🪑 = 2 days

▸ Bar Graph

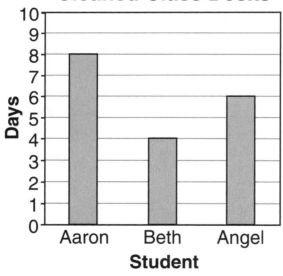

Ask your child to look at the pictograph and identify how many days Aaron cleaned the desks. Make sure your child uses the key. Then, ask your child to identify how many days Beth and Angel cleaned the desks. Finally, point out how this same information is shown in the bar graph.

Second Graders Are...

Second graders are often as interested in getting a peer's assessment or approval of their work as they are of getting their parent's or teacher's assessment or approval. Try to involve your kid's friends or siblings when you do the activities in this book. If possible, have your kid use his or her art or posters to explain an idea to them.

On Your Way to an "A" Activities

15 minutes

Type: Reading/Writing
Materials needed: newspapers, magazines, household items, paper, pencil
Number of players: 2 or more

Play "Charts and Graphs Everywhere!" The goal is to see how many places you can find charts and graphs. Go around your house with the other players looking for charts and graphs. Write the name of the room you are in on a piece of paper. When you find a chart or graph, write a description of it. For example, you might write "Laundry room—chart of how much laundry soap to use for each load." Once you find a chart or graph, move on. Look for at least one chart or graph in every room of your house.

20 minutes

Type: Arts and Crafts
Materials needed: paper, pencil, crayons and markers, glue, macaroni, other art supplies
Number of players: 1 or more

Pretend you own a pet store. You want to find out how many types of fish you have. Draw a picture of a large fish tank with different types of fish (striped fish, red fish, blue fish, and others). You can glue macaroni to the bottom for "sea grass." Then, make a tally chart, pictograph, or bar graph showing the different types of fish you have in your pet store.

Using Your Head

*Grab some **crayons, markers,** and a **pencil!***

Sunshine Pets is a local pet store. The store owner counted how many dogs and cats are in the store. The store owner wants to put this information into a pictograph. Draw the pictograph. Give it a title. Then, color the animals in the pictograph.

Animal	Number
Dogs	~~IIII~~ ~~IIII~~ ~~IIII~~ ~~IIII~~ ~~IIII~~ ~~IIII~~
Cats	~~IIII~~ ~~IIII~~ ~~IIII~~ ~~IIII~~ ~~IIII~~

_____

Key	🐱 or 🐶 = _____ Number of Pets

Range and Mode

Finding the range and mode of a set of numbers is an important skill; range and mode help kids interpret data in charts and graphs. However, second graders sometimes get overwhelmed when asked to deal with many numbers at once. Graphs, charts, ranges, and modes are still new to them, so they may not be comfortable answering questions about them. Instead of seeing information about the lengths of snakes, kids might just see groups of numbers jumbled together and give up.

To be able to find the range and mode of a graph or chart, your kid needs to understand what range and mode are and the differences between them, as well as practice reading charts and graphs. Once your child gets these things down, finding the range and mode won't be so tricky.

First things first: Get a sense of what your kid already knows. Turn the page and tell your kid to Jump Right In!

Here's what you'll need for this lesson:
- *pencil*
- *paper*
- *newspapers*
- *O-shaped cereal (or other small, edible items)*

Jump Right In!

Use this tally chart to answer questions 1 and 2.

Animal	Number
Lions	||||
Elephants	||||
Snakes	~~||||~~ ~~||||~~ |
Tigers	||

1. What is the mode?

   A. 2

   B. 4

   C. 9

   D. 13

2. What is the range?

   A. 2

   B. 4

   C. 9

   D. 13

Use this bar graph for questions 3 and 4.

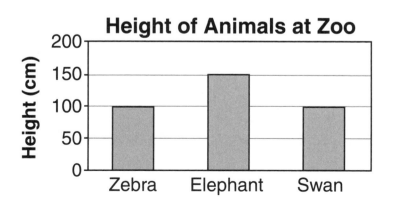

Height of Animals at Zoo

3. What is the range?

    A. 50 centimeters

    B. 100 centimeters

    C. 150 centimeters

    D. 200 centimeters

4. What is the mode?

    A. 50 centimeters

    B. 100 centimeters

    C. 150 centimeters

    D. 200 centimeters

Use this pictograph to answer questions 5 and 6.

Lengths of Reptiles

Salamander	● ● ●
Rattlesnake	● ● ● ● ● ● ● ● ● ● ● ● ● ● ● ● ● ●
Iguana	● ● ● ● ● ● ● ● ● ● ●
Turtle	● ● ●

Key	● = 5 cm

5. What is the range of reptile lengths?

6. What is the mode?

Excellent Job!

Checking In

Answers for pages 254 and 255:

1. B

2. C

3. A

4. B

5. An A+ answer: 85 centimeters

6. An A+ answer: 15 centimeters

Did your child get the correct answers? If so, ask your child to explain the steps he or she took to find the range and mode for each graph.

Did your child get any of the answers wrong? If so, ask, "What does *range* mean? What does *mode* mean?" If your child has difficulty answering, explain that range is the difference between the least and greatest numbers and that the mode is the number that repeats the most often in a set. Then, ask your child to come up with definitions in his or her own words.

Watch Out!

Most second graders are unfamiliar with the terms *range* and *mode*. You probably know that *range* can mean how far something is spread out (like the range of your cell phone signal) or the place where cattle graze (like in "Home, home on the range"). However, most second graders don't know this. Range and mode are abstract words to them, and most kids will probably try to just memorize the definitions instead of really understanding them. Help your kid avoid mixing up the words by using mnemonics. Explain that if you *ran* from the littlest number to the greatest number, you'd find the *range*. Also, tell your child that the word *mode* sounds like *most,* so your child can think of *mode* as being the number that appears the *most* often.

What to Know...

Kids analyze data all the time without realizing it. They may notice that the most popular lunch in school is peanut butter and jelly sandwiches or that their height marks on the wall for the last year went from 4 feet 2 inches to 4 feet 3 inches. Kids just aren't familiar with the terms *mode* and *range* yet.

Review these skills with your child this way:

- The **range** is the difference between the least and greatest numbers in a set of data.
- The **mode** is the number(s) or item(s) that occurs the most often in a set of data.

In school, your kid might make a bar graph showing the heights of his or her classmates. Your kid can find the range of heights.

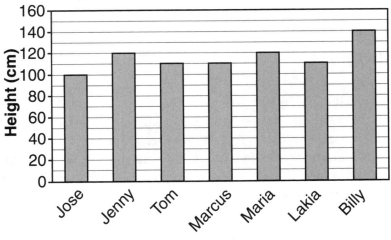

Height of Kids in Mrs. Johnson's Class

Range: 40 cm
Mode: 110 cm

Ask your kid to find the greatest height and the least height. Then, ask your child to subtract the least height from the greatest height to find the range. Explain that finding the range means that you know the difference in heights in the class.

Your kid can also find the height that is the most common by finding the mode.

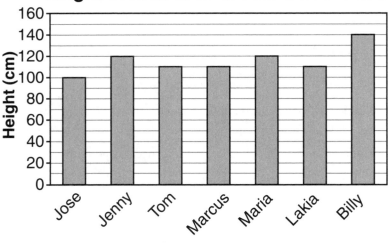

Height of Kids in Mrs. Johnson's Class

Range: 40 cm
Mode: 110 cm

 *Study Right*

Your kid may find it easier to use a bar graph—he or she might be able to see the tallest bar in the graph and shortest bar in the graph more easily than trying to figure out the least and greatest numbers in a set. However, it's helpful for your child to develop the habit of writing data in a set from least to greatest. Encourage your kid to write a list of the heights of each student. Then, ask your kid to order the heights from least to greatest. Now, your kid should be able to easily identify the least height and the greatest height as well as the height that occurs the most often in the set.

· · · · · · · · · · · · · · ●
Point out to your kid that two classmates are 120 centimeters tall (Maria and Jenny) and three classmates are 110 centimeters tall (Tom, Marcus, and Lakia), so 110 is the mode.

On Your Way to an "A" Activities

10 minutes

Type: Speaking/Listening
Materials needed: O-shaped cereal (or other small, edible items)
Number of players: 3 or more

Each player grabs a handful of cereal. Then, each player counts the number of pieces he or she has and tells the others. These three numbers are your data. Together, find the range of these numbers. Then, find the mode. If there is no mode, eat some of the cereal from a set until you have a mode. Talk with the other players to agree on the number of cereal pieces you need to eat to have a mode.

20 minutes

Type: Reading/Writing
Materials needed: newspaper, paper, pencil
Number of people: 1

Look at the sports pages in the newspaper. Find your favorite team or favorite player. Make a chart of information about that team or player. For example, you can make a chart of the points scored in the last bunch of games. Then, find the range and mode of this set of data.

Second Graders Are...

Often, second graders play hard and tire themselves out quickly. Working on one activity at a time may be more effective than working on all the activities during one sitting.

Using Your Head

{20 minutes}

Grab a pencil!

Look at this set of data:

6, 4, 11, 5, 10

Order the numbers from least to greatest. What is the range?

Now, connect the numbers in the set in order from least to greatest to check your answer!

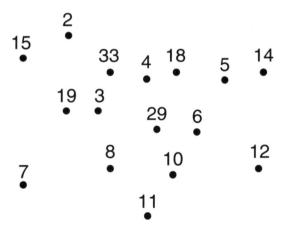

Answer: The range is 7.

Likely or Unlikely

Second graders have lots of favorites. Kids at this age usually have favorite colors, favorite toys, favorite books, favorite shirts, etc., and aren't shy about telling everyone and their dog why their favorites are the best. It's no wonder, then, that kids can have trouble answering questions about the likelihood of events. Who cares what the colors are on the spinner when your favorite color is red?

To figure out if getting red on a spinner is likely or unlikely, your kid needs to learn to disregard his or her own preferences and focus on the given information. Seeing numerous possible outcomes, especially outcomes that they don't like, can be confusing, but kids have to be able to consider all the possible outcomes. Not only will determining if an event is likely or unlikely help kids with their math skills, it will help them with everyday decisions, such as *If the weather forecast is rainy for the whole day, should I bring my umbrella?* and the all important *I like only chocolate chip cookies. Should I eat this mystery cookie from the cookie jar?*

First things first: Get a sense of what your kid already knows. Turn the page and tell your kid to Jump Right In!

Here's what you'll need for this lesson:
- *poster board*
- *markers or crayons*
- *round-head brass fastener or twist-tie*
- *bowl*
- *scissors*
- *index cards*
- *stuffed animals*
- *pencil*
- *paper*

Jump Right In!

1. At a birthday party, everyone gets to pick a balloon from a bag. In the bag, there are 2 red balloons, 1 yellow balloon, 4 blue balloons, and 3 pink balloons. What color balloon is someone unlikely to pick?

   A. red

   B. yellow

   C. blue

   D. pink

Use the picture below to answer questions 2 and 3.

2. Eddie picks a snack from this bag without looking. What is he *likely* to pick?

   A. a pear

   B. a cherry

   C. an apple

   D. a banana

3. Nina picks a snack from this bag without looking. What is she *unlikely* to pick?

   A. a pear

   B. a cherry

   C. an apple

   D. a banana

Johnny and his friends are playing a game with a spinner at his birthday party. Use the spinner below to answer questions 4 and 5.

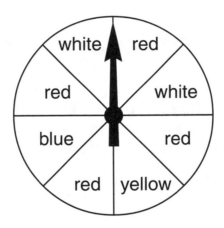

4. Johnny's favorite color is blue. Is it *likely* or *unlikely* that the spinner will land on blue? Why or why not?

5. Kate spins the spinner next. What color will the spinner most *likely* land on? Why?

Excellent Job!

 **Checking In**

🅐Answers for pages 262 and 263:

    1. B

    2. D

    3. A

    4. An A+ answer: It is unlikely that the spinner will land on blue. There is only one part of the spinner that is blue.

    5. An A+ answer: It is likely that the spinner will land on red. There are more red spaces on the spinner than any other color spaces.

Did your child get the correct answers? If so, ask your child to explain how he or she knew the event was likely or unlikely.

Did your child get any of the answers wrong? If so, try acting out a probability question together. Assemble a group of objects, such as 5 pencils, 2 pens, and 9 crayons. Mix them up on the table or in a bag. Ask your child to identify which object occurs most often in the group. Then, ask him to close his eyes and pick out one object. Did he chose a crayon? Talk about why.

 **Watch Out!**

Kids at this age are still developing their vocabularies. Although *likely* and *unlikely* are obvious words to you, make sure your kid understands that *likely* means the event will probably happen (not that she *likes* the event) and *unlikely* means the event will probably not happen. Your kid can write this down to help her throughout the lesson.

 **Study Right**

Encourage your kid to make a habit of explaining his answers. This will make your child think about his thought process and help you see if he really understands a concept or is merely guessing.

What to Know...

Kids may not realize it, but they decide what's *likely* or *unlikely* all the time when playing games and making choices.

Review these skills with your child this way:

- **Likely** means the event will probably occur.
- **Unlikely** means the event will probably not occur.

Your child might find these party hats at a birthday party.

 **Checking In**

Tell your kid to imagine that he or she is at a birthday party and takes a hat without looking. Ask your kid which hat he or she is likely to take and which hat he or she is unlikely to take.

To find out if an event is likely or unlikely, your kid should first figure out how many different hats are in the set. Then, she should figure out how likely she is to choose each hat by counting the number of times it appears in the picture:

- 1 white hat
- 3 polka dot hats
- 3 pink hats
- 7 striped hats

Your child is likely to pick a striped hat because there are many more striped hats than other hats. Your child is unlikely to pick a white hat because that is the hat that occurs least often in the set.

On Your Way to an "A" Activities

Type: Arts and Crafts
Materials needed: poster board, round-head brass fastener or twist-tie, a bowl, markers or crayons, scissors
Number of players: 2 or more

Make your own spinner. Use a bowl or a round object to trace a circle on poster board. Poke a hole at the center of the circle. This will be your spinner. Give it 8 sections, and use 3 or 4 different colors to color the sections. Then, cut an arrow out of poster board and poke a hole through the end. Use the fastener to attach your arrow to the spinner (or slide the twist-tie through the holes).

What color is your spinner likely to land on? Unlikely?

Now, flick the spinner 20 times and record the colors it lands on. Find out if you were right!

Second Graders Are...

At school, students enjoy projects that involve teamwork. Apply this idea at home by including neighbors, friends, and siblings when doing activities. When reviewing examples in this book, change them to include the names of your kid's friends or classmates.

Play "Adventure of the Hidden Treasure." One player is the "Guide," and the other player is the "Adventurer." The Guide hides a stuffed animal somewhere in the room, while the Adventurer closes his or her eyes. Then, the Adventurer must guess the location of the stuffed animal. Each time the Adventurer wants to guess a location, the Guide asks a question about *likely* or *unlikely*. If the Adventurer answers correctly, he or she gets to look in one place. Keep playing until the Adventurer finds the stuffed animal. Then, switch roles.

You can use the *likely* and *unlikely* questions below.

1. At lunch, there is a box of fruit with 2 apples, 1 orange, and 4 bananas.

    What is a kid *likely* to pick? (a banana)

    What is a kid *unlikely* to pick? (an orange)

2. A kid gets to pick a prize at a fair. The bag of prizes contains 1 kazoo, 3 glow-in-the-dark bracelets, and 5 pairs of sunglasses.

    What is a kid *likely* to pick? (a pair of sunglasses)

    What is a kid *unlikely* to pick? (a kazoo)

3. Mrs. Riggs wants something from her purse. In her purse, she has 1 pen, 4 pencils, and 3 packs of gum.

    What is she *likely* to pick? (a pack of gum)

    What is she *unlikely* to pick? (a pen)

Using Your Head

Grab a **pencil**!

Johnny, Kate, and Terry are playing a game.

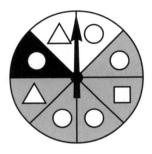

1. Johnny wants to get a square. Is it *likely* or *unlikely* that he'll get a square when he spins the spinner? _____

2. Kate needs to get either pink or black. What is *likely* or *unlikely*? Circle your answer.

   Pink: *likely*   *unlikely*

   Black: *likely*   *unlikely*

3. Terry wants to get a circle. Is it *likely* or *unlikely* that he'll get a circle when he spins the spinner?

Answers: 1. unlikely; 2. Pink is likely and black is unlikely; 3. likely